Stalin BY EMIL LUDWIG

Yes! To this thought I hold with firm persistence;
The last result of wisdom stamps it true:
He only earns his freedom and existence,
Who daily conquers it anew. GOETHE

G. P. PUTNAM'S SONS   NEW YORK

COPYRIGHT, 1942, BY EMIL LUDWIG

Translated by Mrs. Erna McArthur

Designed by Robert Josephy

MANUFACTURED IN THE UNITED STATES OF AMERICA

STALIN

DK
268
S8
L78

CONTENTS

50

Preface

Two circumstances make it difficult in the year 1942 to depict Stalin. He stands in the fourth act of his drama, and nobody knows what is going to happen in the fifth. Besides, he conceals decisive documents which will reveal many things at a later time. It is the more captivating to merge, through that intuition which always is and remains the best source of historical presentation, the facts actually known with those still unknown.

As I have often been attacked in Russia and rarely translated, I am free to stand for the Soviet principles, as I have affirmed it since 1917. Though an unconditional individualist and therefore not a communist, I am irresistibly attracted by the social justice of that world. Though I am convinced that the power of personality is greater than that of numbers and I cannot be taken for a Marxist, the foundation of the Soviet Union appears to me as the greatest event produced by our century till today. The Russians are the only people that have broken the reign of money.

In this independent position I have not hidden my sympathy with Trotsky nor my criticism of the Moscow terrorism—not even before Stalin himself. I visited him a decade before his present victories and publicly expressed my admiration for his great work.

A thoughtless fashion has taken pleasure in pairing Fascism and communism, rejecting both because they make use of similar methods. In reality their spiritual contrast is fundamental and greater than that between each of them and democracy. The constitution of the Soviet Union collects the most forcible arguments of the future, while the program of the Nazis tries to vivify dead thoughts of the Middle Ages.

Stalin is so outstanding as colonizer and general that he towers above most of our contemporary leaders—no matter what his end is going to be. Probably he will be the only dictator who survives the war. Who fears that Stalin's victory will bring world revolution is not aware of the fact that we are in it already.

I am indebted to the excellent works of Max Werner, Isaac Don Levine, Louis Fischer, Walter Duranty, Henry C. Wolfe and Johnson, Dean of Canterbury; further, to the help of H. W. Meyer, New York.

Santa Monica, California
July, 1942   LUDWIG

STALIN

Portrait Sketch

   A writer who deals with living personalities still in the midst of their careers suffers from one definite disadvantage as compared with the historian of the past; at the same time he enjoys a definite advantage over him.

On the one hand, he must do without a great many documents, particularly of the private kind. If I have before me the love letters of a man who has been dead a hundred years I can get to know him much more intimately than one who has left behind him only state documents, however copious. In revolutionary times like ours there is a certain offset to this disadvantage; party members fall away, or are ousted, and if they manage to escape they publish their revelations from the security of exile. Stalin has eliminated most of his opponents, but a few of them are still alive and vocal.

On the other hand, a living personality gives us the opportunity of personal contact, and those of us who have the habit of thinking with our eyes exploit this opportunity to the full. It was for this reason that I sought out

COLD AND ALIEN

Stalin in the Kremlin at a time when he was seeing very few Europeans. Once you have studied a man through his public documents, a visit, especially if it is private, comfortable and unhurried, does more than a hundred pictures to open him up to you. The modulations of his voice, the expression on his face, his smile, his astonishment, his gestures, the movements of his lips, the reflexes of his eyes—it is through these that we penetrate to the soul of a man. When a man comes to you for the first time on a business matter, you immediately form a picture of his personality. This is even truer of our first contact with a woman, the uncertain prelude to any one of an infinite range of emotional possibilities.

The rulers of mankind, whom the ancient world calls heroes, and whom we of today call dictators or presidents, are themselves human beings, precisely like the most obscure of their servants or soldiers; their actions therefore become more intelligible to the student of human nature if he can observe them at first hand with his eyes and ears.

Stalin—we may well say it at the outset—makes a cold and alien impression; there is nothing about him that attracts. He does not come halfway to meet you; he is not open; he is cautious, unresponsive, and, for the most part, somber. When he laughs, it is with a grim, dark laughter, which comes up from the depths. Among the rulers of our time—and I have seen most of them—he is the most impenetrable. Everything about him, speech, walk, gesture, is slow and heavy. There is nothing to indicate trust in men or friendship for them.

4

But this heaviness of Stalin's, which expresses itself in his features, his bearing, and his enunciation, has equipped him with two qualities of immense usefulness in his career: self-certainty and patience. In contrast to Hitler, who is nothing but nerves, Stalin is the man without nerves. He has his patience to thank for his rise to power; for among the four dictators of our time he is the only one who worked his way up slowly.

The others, Hitler, Mussolini and Franco, were the makers of their own revolutions; Stalin was not in the first rank of his revolution. The others conquered power; Stalin inherited it from Lenin. Patience and endurance were therefore primary factors for him, while imagination played no rôle at all.

This persistence gradually prepared the victory for his work. His energy is not of the explosive, lightninglike variety; it is slow and cumulative. That is why he has been able to succeed where his most gifted rivals failed.

It is only by understanding the springs and origins of this strange character that we can grasp the good and evil of his actions.

But you should always have before you the picture of an ordinary man, a plebeian without pose, uncommunicative by nature, even embarrassed by strangers—a man of medium height in a gray, military mantle, who seldom meets the gaze of his interlocutor. The forehead is low, the hair, growing down close, is barely touched with gray, the mouth, which sometimes holds a pipe, close-locked. The reader must think of this man's voice as quiet; the manner of delivery, in the answering of questions, utterly serene and self-confident. Stalin is firm and logical, but no argument can move him even to reconsider his views.

A visitor entering the inner courtyard of the Kremlin—an elevated fortress in the middle of the Bolshevik metropolis, Moscow—is greeted by thousands of cannons turned toward the red battlements. When I went to the Kremlin I was stopped by a guard at the old drawbridge. He asked my name, and the soldier at his side checked it with his book. No document was demanded. I might have been any kind of murderer.

Going through the gate, I passed through three very simply furnished rooms, over a carpet with wide red borders that led to Stalin's door. What is his room like? It is long, but without the slightest touch of that pomp with which Mussolini and Hitler try to impress visitors. At the far end a medium-sized man in a light-brown coat rises from his chair. He is dressed with painful neatness, just as his room is arranged with the accuracy of a doctor's consulting room. There is a large table in the middle on which are set plain water carafes, plain glasses and ash trays, all in apple-pie order. The walls are dark green. On them hang large photographs of Lenin and Marx. On Stalin's desk there are a photograph of Lenin and five telephones such as I find all dictators use for certain purposes.

During my three hours' visit (December 1931) Stalin practically never looked at me but kept on drawing figures on paper with a red pencil, the blue end of which he never used. He was filling many sheets and tearing them up.

AN ASIATIC

When I mentioned the name of Trotsky he was drawing a ship. Suddenly he looked at me. It was a dour look, the veiled glance of a lonely and suspicious man who by nature and experience was distrustful. I could imagine him suddenly rising, advancing slowly toward his opponent, and looking him straight in the eye. This plodding man is capable of surprise.

As he talks, Stalin lets syllables fall like heavy hammer blows. His answers are short and clear, not those of a man who oversimplifies things before a public audience, but those of a logical thinker whose mind works slowly and without the least emotion. For twelve years this man has made all his decisions alone. He will never take advice. He decides, orders, acts, without words. He is the most silent man I ever saw, silent until he suddenly rises to attack you. This silence, this slowness, show him an Asiatic.

At the head of his dinner table, in a little room, sits a man of sixty-two whose green-gray coat is military only in its cut. Face, habits, manner of speech differentiate him from no worker. He eats in silence. His wife, forty years old, like himself was of proletarian birth and dressed with the utmost simplicity. The children of fifteen and twenty, who attend public schools, are perhaps telling a story they heard in the city; now and again they laugh, now and again the father grunts something approvingly. The food comes from the Kremlin kitchen, which provides in exactly the same way for hundreds of officials. A soldier brought it over, and now hands in the dishes.

The comical legend that Stalin eats off the golden plate

of the Czars, and the other one, printed and reprinted hundreds of times in the west, that he spends 100,000 rubles a year on himself, are totally lacking in imagination. A lower-middle-class parvenu like Goering must have castles, fanfares of trumpets to herald the entry of his guests, and a liveried lackey behind every chair at the dinner table. A frenzied dreamer like Hitler must have a tower with a glass cupola in which to brood on world dominion in Wagnerian mood. A pint-size Roman hero like Mussolini must have the largest Renaissance room extant, so that from a desk in the corner of this hall he may play the universal ruler.

Stalin, the man who thinks in percentages, horsepower, and volts, has created a much more fantastic legend: the story of a shoemaker's son who in the seat of the Czar still lives like a shoemaker. The castle itself he never enters, and if he lives in the official quarters which tower above the old walls of the Kremlin, it is only that the people may perceive in him the symbol of the inheritance of power. If he has ever happened to see, in the near-by museum, the golden coronation carriage of the Czars, he did not feel the slightest impulse to imitate the ancient rulers, as do the dictators of the west who must display their power in interminable processions.

Unlike Hitler, he feels no need to take revenge either for his lowly origin or for a lost youth. Stalin's youth was not lost; it stood for the same idea as his mature years; he was never afflicted with a feeling of inferiority in the presence of the rich and the mighty. As against this, Hitler's political activity, indeed his entire life, is nothing other than one long revenge on those who were born to greater advantages. That is why he hates the rich, the fortunate, the healthy; and most violently he hates the Americans, because in a thousand pictures he sees them forever laughing—something forbidden to him. Stalin, too, laughs little, for he is an Asiatic, but he can make fun of the deposed class because he does not imitate it.

In the summer, when the family lives in Gorki in the little country house which Lenin occupied toward the end, Stalin may feel more strongly his rôle as Lenin's successor than in the wintry Kremlin. In Gorki he can go fishing and hunting, pursuits which these revolutionaries all acquired in exile. This is a healthy, moderate man who in fifteen years of rule has never manifested a single symptom of delusions of grandeur. He does not wear on his left sleeve or his right trouser leg any of the insignia which are the delight of dictators. He is certainly the only dictator who wears no necktie.

A friend of his told me that he does not permit anyone to tell smutty stories in his presence. He has married twice, and that is the whole of his private life. Like all old soldiers, he likes to reminisce over adventures which ended happily. Almost the only foreigner who ever cracked jokes with him was the American engineer Cooper, who won his confidence by the building of the Dnieper Dam. Bernard Shaw, too, told me that he laughed a great deal with Stalin; but then, who does not laugh with Bernard Shaw?

I heard Stalin laugh only once in that heavy way of his.

After a conversation lasting for several hours, he called on me, if I felt so inclined, to donate some money for poor children in Germany, "since you are going to make money out of our conversation!" I was staggered, and replied, "I thought communists were opposed to charity." At this point he laughed and said: "Among ourselves! But in your capitalist countries it is unfortunately still natural." Later I had a Berlin committee send to the Kremlin the receipt of my donation, to let him know that I had not wriggled out of it. It was just an ironical dig on his part, intended to embarrass the bourgeois.

Let us put three words next to each other which characterize him from different viewpoints:

"The art of leadership is a serious matter," Stalin wrote in 'thirty after he had become dictator. "One must not straggle behind a movement, nor run in front of it, lest one becomes—in both cases—separated from the masses. Whoever wants to lead, and at the same time maintain his contact with the masses, must fight on two fronts: against those loitering in the rear, and those speeding on ahead."

To his Ambassador in Tokio Stalin said: "I am no diplomat and give you no instructions. Only this: Tell the Japanese as little as possible and cable us as much as possible. And don't believe that you are cleverer than other people."

At another time, while drinking wine in company with two old leaders, he raised the question what each man considered the best thing in his life. This happened in

'24, when the tension between him and Trotsky was already great. Then Stalin said: "The best thing in life is to ferret out one's enemy, prepare the stroke carefully, revenge oneself mercilessly, and then lie down to sleep."

CHAPTER ONE

Flight from the Priests

The house in which Stalin was born stands in a little town in the Caucasus. It looks much more wretched than the cabin Lincoln was born in, for the natural logs of the latter at least remind us of the man's hands that cut them and put them together. Stalin's birthplace is a miserable brick cottage with four tiny rooms; one side is glazed over, the top being nailed down with boards of unequal length; the threshold consists of a tilted stone, over which people undoubtedly used to stumble sixty-two years ago, when the mother gave birth to this boy. I saw the old woman once, in 1925, in Tiflis; she was returning, after a stroll, to a very simple apartment house; earnest and careworn, she wore the dark veil which was customary with the women of the region; she was obviously as indifferent to wealth and the joys of life as her son, from whom, as the master of two hundred million people, she could have demanded and obtained everything.

Mothers are perhaps the most moving figures which surround the man of power, for they pray every night not for power, but for the life which they brought forth. The heroic mothers who were prepared to see their sons die in the name of glory were undoubtedly rarer, even in the antique world, than legend would have us believe. In our day, when kings are disappearing and three plebeians rule a large section of the earth, the pathos of such a family is not to be found in the purple and magnificence of royalty; we must look for it in the sorrowful lines of an old woman's face, and in the pain-filled eyes which express nothing but a mother's love.

In the pitiful brick hut that cost one and a half rubles in rent, this cobbler's wife managed to give two hours a day to cooking and housework; for she was herself a worker, and her husband, who was later employed in a shoe factory, was not a peasant, as Russian children are told today regarding Stalin's father. Like most of his neighbors, he had a little garden, and sometimes a cow and a few chickens. It was there that the boy got his first meager tuition; but the sphere of his childhood was wholly and entirely that of the proletariat, which possesses nothing—neither land, nor tradition, nor God, nor hope.

What must be the first emotions of a twelve-year-old wide-awake boy in such surroundings? What does he see in front of him, to envy and desire? His father tells him that he himself was born a slave, for slavery was abolished in the Caucasus almost in the same year as in America. The word in use was not slavery, but ownership—it came to the same thing. It was abolished there not by a great war, but by an act of grace on the part of an invisible Czar, who reigned a thousand miles away, and a thousand miles above the clouds; the great landlords, however, remained where they had always been, very close at hand, and continued to treat their peasants like cattle—that is, unless their emotions underwent a sudden change in the Russian manner, and they came to sit in their servants' huts, and to drink tea with them, holding a piece of sugar between the teeth and sucking the tea in through it.

What was there in such an environment to console or inspire a half-neglected boy? It would have been far more natural for him to become a pauper than a statesman, for there were many conditions which pointed to the former, and none at all to the latter.

In this land of Georgia, which lies in the southern Caucasus between the Black and Caspian seas, only a well-fed, well-clad youth, who goes to a bright, clean school, looks at maps and models, and plays daily on a beautiful sports field, can learn to appreciate and admire the wild mountains of the region. The towering summits, higher than those of the Alps, remind one of the magnificent peaks of Mexico. Given food and sleep enough, given the right teachers, he could also have studied, in his native land, a whole swarm of races, Georgians, Armenians, Kurds, Turks, Jews, and many other intertwined with them, so that it is ridiculous to try to determine the race Stalin belongs to. In the markets and bazaars of Tiflis, near by, a wide-awake boy who used his eyes could learn to distinguish many of these races, as well as Mohammedans and various

Christian sects; he could also observe the churches and the mosques, and a motley, colorful life which puts the western visitor in mind of Smyrna or Cairo.

But all this remained a sealed book to the ill-clad, ill-fed proletarian boy. His passion—for Stalin's fiber glows through and through with a dark fire such as must be kindled in a man's earliest years—could direct itself against two things which surrounded his visions and desires with hostile denial: the people and the class which ruled over him and his parents.

The feelings evoked by these two phenomena differed widely from each other. The Georgians, an old cultural people, who can be compared with the Spanish nobility for pride and quixotism, were on good terms with the Russians, being linked to them by religion. The Russo-Caucasian war had been waged only against the local Mohammedan mountain tribes. But the Georgians had always been the weaker party, and had had to accept the leadership of the so-called Great Russians, that is, of the rulers of Moscow and St. Petersburg. Militarily weaker than the Russians, but culturally stronger—which they are even today—the Georgians stood toward the Russians more or less as the Austrians did toward the Prussians. Stalin's impulse toward Greater Russia was like Hitler's toward Prussia.

In the Caucasus, as in the rest of Russia, a handful of the nobility, not more than a couple of thousand in all, lived and enjoyed life at the expense of the other classes. These Junkers, whose particular delight it was to spend the income from their Georgian estates in the Rue de Rivoli, in Paris, were protected in their hereditary possession by the troops of the Czar, for it was their support which, in turn, maintained the Czar. More than one imperial ruler had been murdered by the nobility. What could such a despot, supposing he felt for the hundred million peasants whom he ruled, do in opposition to the interests of a hundred thousand landed proprietors?

Even the smaller landowners—they called themselves princes in the Caucasus if their possessions consisted of half a dozen acres of land and twice as many cows—had to be protected by the Czarist machinery of state. There was one universal law: the peasants had to be kept, in poverty and ignorance, at the bottom of the pyramid.

For in reality it was the peasant who, owning nothing, worked eighty-five per cent of the land. Who would have dared to prophesy, in the days of slavery, or even as little as thirty years ago, that the time was coming when the peasants would own their own land, or lease it from the state, that half of this immense empire would be industrialized, and that there would be no more counts and princes? A transformation of such rapidity occurs very rarely in history.

Ideas of this order cannot have have occurred to the boy growing up in poverty and ignorance; still less could he have dreamed that he would play a decisive rôle in the transformation.

Whenever the lad questioned his father, whenever he read the newspaper for himself, or whenever he looked around him in Tiflis and saw the glittering squads of Cossacks, the opulent three-in-hand coaches of the nobility, or a Circassian princess in her pointed shoes stepping down from her carriage to slip into the waiting door of a palace, he had immediately before him the second object of his hatred. The aim and purpose of his whole life were already fixed for this defiant boy when he was thirteen years old: they were directed against the Georgians, against the rich. Since neither religion nor philosophy provided the counterbalance in his soul, his first drive was bound to be destructive.

At this point his mother intervened. Enlisting the help of a relative, the poor cobbler's wife succeeded in enrolling the obviously wide-awake youngster in an Orthodox religious seminary in Tiflis, where he would receive his board and lodging and be prepared for the priesthood. Perhaps the mother was religiously inclined; there is a touch of religion in every Slav. Concerning the views on God and destiny which Stalin expressed to me, I shall speak further on.

When the fourteen-year-old boy entered the seminary at his mother's wish, to train for the priesthood, he did not, like Luther, disappear into a monastic cell. The Russian spirit had been in a state of turmoil and revolt for at least a century, and it was inevitable that the same condition should be found in the religious schools. Twenty years before, there had already been revolts and clashes in this particular seminary. On one occasion the Rector had fulminated against the Georgian language, whereupon a student had stood up and knocked him down. Some time later a nineteen-year-old student stabbed an archbishop, and a subsequent report from Tiflis to the Holy Synod recorded that one-half of the student body applauded the murder. Stalin was by no means the first to come to grief in this seminary.

But he was obviously the first to become a Socialist via a training for the priesthood. President Masaryk of Czechoslovakia, the son of an imperial coachman, once told me that at the age of six he was already a Socialist at heart because of the contemptuous attitude of the Bohemian counts toward his father. But, when I asked Stalin whether the privations of his childhood had made him what he was, he answered in the negative and offered me the following astonishing explanation:

"My parents had no education, but they did much for me. Such things as you tell me about Masaryk did not make me into a Socialist, either at the age of six or at the age of twelve. I became one at the seminary, because the character of the discipline enraged me. The place was a hotbed of espionage and chicanery. At nine in the morning we assembled for tea, and when we returned to our bedrooms all the drawers had been rifled. And just as they went daily through our papers, they went daily through our souls. I could not stand it; everything infuriated me. And at that time the first illegal groups of Russian Socialists were coming to the Caucasus. They made a deep impression on me, and I immediately acquired a taste for forbidden literature."

19

It appears that the boy learned little about religion at the seminary but much about singing, for we find reference to him as a sort of cantor or prayer leader; and once, on the Czar's birthday, he rendered a solo in an Orthodox church and won a medal for it. How grotesque are the stories which come to us out of the boyhood of revolutionaries!

At that time Stalin took his first step into that internationalism which was destined to determine his later life: exchanging lessons with a schoolmate from some unpronounceable locality in western Asia, he mastered the foreign dialect, while the other boy learned the Georgian language.

But the most important thing then taken up by Stalin was debating, this typically Russian means for clarifying, comparing, and defining one's thoughts. The following is an account later given by a fellow pupil in an evidently slightly dramatized version: "One morning I met Stalin, surrounded by his schoolmates, on the Pushkin square. We were all excited over various leaflets and articles which one or the other had ferreted out. Somebody mentioned the name of Tulin, whose article we had secretly read. But we knew that this was the pseudonym of an exiled writer who sometimes called himself also Lenin. Stalin listened and said: 'I must meet this man!' The school bell dispersed the boys. Later we tore the only copy of Marx's *Das Kapital* to be found in Tiflis out of each other's hands."

When four years had passed, the eighteen-year-old Stalin was expelled from the seminary. We may well imagine what this meant to the mother, who had hoped to secure her son's future. Her sense of honor was wounded, too, so that even in her old age she denied the expulsion; and while journalists and biographers in Russia dwelt with pride on this incident in Stalin's life, one voice was lifted to me in protest. Long after her son had become dictator—she was already close to the eighties—his mother explained vigorously:

"No, he was not expelled. I brought him home because of his health. When he entered the seminary, he was fresh and strong. But he studied too much, and the doctor said he might become consumptive. That's why I took him away. He would have been glad to stay on, but I took him back. He was my only son, a good boy; I never had to punish him. No, he wasn't expelled!"

This touching falsehood—which the old woman undoubtedly accepted as the gospel truth—was not intended to demonstrate her share in the revolutionary molding of her son. She only wanted to defend the honor of the family. So completely do the next of kin misunderstand the mission of an extraordinary man.

Where are we, in Europe or in Asia? This question was already raised by the geographers of antiquity, Herodotus and Strabo, when they spoke of the Caucasus. Traversing a lofty Caucasian mountain pass by car, I was delighted beyond measure by the sight of a signpost with two arms, on which was painted, in Russian characters: "To Europe!" "To Asia!" The year was 1925; our automobile traveled for the most part on three wheels, the radiator became overheated every fifteen minutes, the engine had to take periodic rests from sheer exhaustion, while the driver poked about in its interior with a piece of wire. I was ready to believe that I was in Asia.

The mountains hereabouts are gloomy and magnificent, though the peaks lack the clarity of outline and the articulation of the Swiss Alps. Here everything is overdone, oppressive, and wild. Stalin undoubtedly learned at school that it was in his native land that Odysseus visited the Troglodytes, whose cave dwellings may still be seen not far from the city of Tiflis. Jewish legend designates the Caucasus mountains as the last resting place of Noah's ark, while the Greeks consign to their care the *Argo* on which Jason and his companions sought the golden fleece. Young Stalin cannot have cared much about either. But, when he learned that Prometheus of old was chained to one of these rocks, he may have paused long enough on the story to wonder whether the demigod ever succeeded in slipping his chains and escaping: for slipping his chains was to become an important preoccupation of this much captured and recaptured revolutionary.

Yes, it was Asia, and it is only as an Asiatic figure that Stalin can be understood. Everything about the young man now emerging slowly is Asiatic; and it will always remain Asiatic: the slow persistence, the silent consistency, the coldness. That which we designate as typically Georgian, but which happens to be Russian, is the exact opposite. We know that from a number of famous novels, but also from history and legend. The typical Russian character is fundamentally more good-natured, softer; it is capable of murder one wild instant, and of sobbing remorse the next. Lenin admitted to Maxim Gorky how he suffered when he had to invoke the reign of terror during the civil war in order to save the Revolution. We may be quite sure that he did not weep with his eyes, but with his heart.

In contrast to him, Stalin, the Georgian and Caucasian, whose home is on the farther side of the signpost where the road goes southward, is closer, in the very formation of his eyes, to the Mongolian type. His heart probably did not weep, when he had several of his oldest comrades executed for high treason; he doubtless slept well at night. Let us compare the dictators. Stalin is four years older than Mussolini and ten years older than Hitler, one year older than Trotsky and nine years younger than Lenin.

Let us compare the picture of the twenty-two-year-old Stalin with those of the other two dictators at his age, and we already perceive the difference in their characters and even a forecast of their respective futures—one which is perhaps more important than the astrological variety.

Before his twenty-first year Mussolini was too poor to have himself photographed; he revenged himself, as a friend of his said to me, by later becoming the most photographed man of his age. But pictures of him as a young Socialist and teacher show us a glowing face from which a fiery spirit looks out upon the world. He did not yet have the head of an aging Roman emperor, nor was there yet any trace of violence in it. Hitler, who at the same age is presented to us as a soldier with long mustache, strikes us as heavily hysterical, pale, uncertain, searching.

Of Stalin at the age of twenty-two we have two pictures, taken at the same time; between them they give us the man. On the profile photograph we see him with a sparse, loose sailor beard, a large mane, thoughtful expression, and a soft artist's tie, so that he looks like an idealist who could also write poetry, or think up a new philosophy. But in full face, with his black mustache, his dark coat, the blinking expression, he looks like a conspirator. The line of his life runs between these polar extremes; it followed an ideal, but it never shrank from violence in order to reach its goal. Of the three dictators, Stalin, with his patience and his distrust, is perhaps in the long run the strongest. That second photograph has no parallel to it among any of the revolutionary rulers of our time.

Having attained power more slowly than the others, he has a firmer grip on it. To accuse such a man of ambition is to be ignorant of the psychology of the strong; for without ambition we should have few great men, and these only among thinkers and artists. Without ambition the active life would wither away completely. Rivalry, competition, the keen desire to win the game, is inborn in man, and we have reason to doubt the puritan's pure objective desire to help the fatherland or humanity.

But while Mussolini and Hitler, and naturally our two great democratic leaders also, are driven forward by the thought of fame, Stalin is entirely devoid of the emotion of pathos, and wants nothing better than loneliness, so that he can mold his power entirely according to his plans. None of these men has the slightest feeling for money; but Stalin has not even the slightest feeling for personal surroundings. His room in the Kremlin, to which I shall shortly introduce the reader, looks like a cold office. All the things needed by Hitler and Mussolini for their receptions and public appearances are utterly alien to Stalin, as they were to Lenin.

When this young Asiatic threw himself into the thankless and dangerous petty tasks of the illegal parties—the Socialist first, and then the Bolshevik—he still spoke a broken Russian; it was only much later, when he had passed his thirtieth year, that he learned something like the proper pronunciation. The fact that he was not a Russian gave a special impetus to his early activity. Napoleon, the Corsican, gave himself up to France, the country which his forefathers had always hated, and which he, too, had hated in his boyhood, because it had conquered his native land. Pilsudski, the half-Lithuanian, gave himself up to Poland out of a similar feeling. As an oppressed Austrian, Hitler, who is only strong in hate, chose the hated and yet admired oppressor, Prussia, as the country he would rule. Out of such conquests there arise, as in the love struggle between men and women, sudden and unexpected emotions of love: then the victorious dictator is like the happy conqueror of a woman. That is why Napoleon later loved France. Pilsudski, Hitler, and Stalin became the sons of their adopted countries when they became their fathers.

But among these five men only the one hysteric, Hitler, is driven by his perversity to dishonor and destroy his own countrymen, the Austrians, whereas the others have always had a protective attitude toward their first homeland. Stalin has always retained, and frequently expressed, a special regard for Georgia. But when it came to political matters, he put down ruthlessly the revolt of his native land—in 1922 and 1924; he was even rebuked for this by Lenin, before the latter's death.

During the decade between his twentieth and thirtieth years Stalin, with his unpronounceable name, was not yet Stalin, but Sosso, Kuba, and half a dozen other aliases, for he and his comrades were in perpetual flight from the Czarist police. The Okhrana, which also had several names, was the prototype of the organization which Stalin later built up as the G.P.U., and the model for Himmler's Gestapo. The Czars were the real discoverers of the system, just as refined torture was the discovery of the fanatical Middle Ages into which the tortures of a modern Inquisition are trying to transform our enlightened era.

It is difficult to reconstruct the early life of Stalin from documents; a man who leads this kind of existence always burns his letters, destroys the minutes of meetings and even obliterates his footsteps; so that one can hardly apply to him Longfellow's admonition to leave "footprints in the sands of time." The political propaganda of Stalin's later years had little material to falsify concerning his earlier years. All that his opponents want to prove is, that until the time of the Revolution, when he was thirty-eight years old, Stalin had not attracted great attention. This, however, is entirely in keeping with his character, for even if he did entertain, at that time, dreams of a great career, it was part of his Asiatic nature to conceal them completely from his comrades.

At twenty-three he was arrested for the first time. This happened in Batum. Later he came to know a dozen jails, while Mussolini wandered eleven times from one prison to the next. During this first experience Stalin immediately sought to come in contact with other political prisoners. One of them describes the incident in this way:

"Our first efforts were without success. Later I learned that a fellow countryman of mine delivered wood to the prison. He and his mate, a driver called Mikh, agreed to get me into the prison yard as a worker who stacked the wood. The next thing to do was to find out at what hour Stalin was let out to exercise so that we could bring our wood in at that time.

"At the prison gate there was a vegetable stand kept by a Persian. He was allowed into the yard once a day to sell fruit to the prisoners. By chance I found out that he had a brother working at my factory. His brother turned out to be well inclined to us. Through this brother we got the vegetable seller to find out when Stalin would be in the yard and to give him a message.

"The day arrived; I did my wood stacking as slowly as possible. The prisoners walked up and down the yard while the guard stood in the center. Every time Stalin passed me he uttered a few quick words—instructions for the work of our organization. In this way we kept up our work even while Stalin was in prison.

"During one of my visits to the prison yard he dropped a paper at my feet. I picked it up. It was a manifesto to the Batum oil workers. When our workers read the manifesto, they were amazed how well Stalin knew the life and needs of the workers. He put forward the demands for each separate trade. The manifesto was of great importance, for it helped weld the workers together."

This much is definite: between 1903 and 1913 Stalin, under his various names, was captured six times by the police, and six times sent to Siberia. He invariably escaped. To be sure, a Czarist prisoner found it easier to slip his chains than a Prometheus. The utter disintegration of the Czarist state machine may be gauged from the fact that while it maintained an expensive system of spies, detectives, and stool pigeons, it was never capable of keeping its captured enemies under lock and key.

The immense disorderliness of Russia, which the Bolsheviks have been combating for twenty years, was no less evident in the administration of the empire than in the soul of its subjects. Here is a people which has little of the dramatic but much of the dithyrambic in its soul; hence its drama is poor, its choreography superb. Just as ferocity and tenderness lie next to each other in the Russian soul, so we find condemned revolutionaries being sent, generation after generation, to Siberia, and often being treated with great kindness by their guards! The concentration camp was quite unknown under the Czars. Siberia is a vast and beautiful country, very cold in the winter, very hot in the summer. Since many of the deportees were writers, we have vivid reports which contain few complaints. The writers seem to have lacked nothing except the field of their activities.

Stalin is among those who were able to catch up, in exile, with the reading which his agitated life of propaganda made impossible. More than that, a man who is inclined to go fishing and hunting every day can build his health up admirably in Siberia. Stalin, who nearly developed tuberculosis in his youth, cured himself of the predisposition out in Siberia. The sudden and terrible ice wind which sweeps across the steppes, the Buran, as it is called, once got him in its grip as he was crossing a frozen river. He struggled against it for hours before he reached a peasant hut. The inmates took him for a ghost. He collapsed on the threshold; he was taken in and warmed; he slept for eight hours, and from that time on was free from the danger of tuberculosis.

In Siberia Stalin also did something for the completion of his education, and in this he resembles Mussolini, who told me with considerable satisfaction of the reading he managed to do in his eleven prisons. It appears that the Czar, intent on the destruction of his enemies, only succeeded in setting them up, physically and mentally. Stalin got his first real understanding of Karl Marx, who had been studied by Russian intellectuals for nearly three generations, in the peacefulness of his Siberian exiles. In the records of the revolutionaries there are descriptions of charming scenes: prisoners reading Karl Marx's *Kapital* to their Cossack guards; the latter fall asleep in sheer boredom, the former stay only too wide awake.

Until the time of the Revolution the Russians avoided all discipline, and in the course of sixty years lost three great wars in a row; in this vaguely governed, shapeless, immense empire there was a sort of ladder on which the illegal mounted step by step to legality. You could always find revolutionaries among counts, upstarts among workers, and stool pigeons, ready to betray their own flesh and blood, in all classes.

The masses whom the young propagandist and his colleagues had to work on, had been drawn in large numbers to the oil wells of Baku, which were first developed in the seventies of the last century; by the beginning of the twentieth century, hundreds of thousands of workers, in a great mixture of races and religions, were already concentrated there. Living in their miserable tin-sheet huts and hovels, they were excellent material for the socialist movement. There Stalin passed that laborious and obscure third decade of his life, returning again and again from Siberia to take up the labor of unifying the workers: an interminable series of lectures, demonstrations, leaflets, pamphlets, spreading enlightenment and revolt.

But half of Stalin's struggle, perhaps more than half, was not directed against the Czar, but against other workers' parties. From early youth he came to know the warfare inside his own class, the passionate antagonism of sects against each other. His whole life—especially the dark epochs to which he sacrificed a part of his constructive period—the entire development of his character can only be understood if one visualizes this ceaseless strife with comrades who had the same goal but wanted to rebuild state and society in other ways.

Already in Baku, just before the revolution of 1905, Stalin wrote, spoke, and agitated passionately against the Mensheviks, Anarchists, and Social Revolutionaries—all of them related movements which stirred him deeper than the Czar. In his youth he always belonged to the most radical Left, soon assuming leadership in the Caucasus. Illustrating his activities and the firm consistency of his position, which won him the confidence of the workers, is this episode recalled by one of the participants:

"On October 17, 1905, the frightened Czar issued a manifesto promising democratic liberties and the convocation of a legislative assembly. The Bolsheviks warned us that the manifesto was a trap; the Mensheviks hailed it and said we had won everything. At one of our meetings Comrade Koba (Stalin's party name at that time) said: 'You have a bad habit; let's be frank about it. No matter who the speaker is, no matter what he says, you have the same welcome for everyone; and you applaud everything said. When the speaker shouts 'long live liberty,' you applaud; when another cries 'long live the revolution,' you applaud. When a speaker tells you 'down arms' you applaud, too. But what revolution can win without arms; and what kind of revolutionist is it who shouts 'down arms'? Whoever he may be, that man is an enemy of the revolution.' The meeting took life from these words. Koba stepped from the platform before a cheering crowd."

At that time Stalin himself wrote: "Formerly our Party resembled a hospitable patriarchal family, and was ready to accept all sympathizers into its midst. But now that our Party has become a centralized *organization,* it has thrown off its patriarchal aspect and has come in all respects to resemble a fortress, whose gates are opened only to the worthy."

Plots and Pursuits

   The basic idea of the system derived from Marx, but it was first adapted for Russia by Lenin: there can be no liberation of the peasants without the leadership of the workers! It was among the city masses, the factory workers, the own-nothings, that the Revolution was to be prepared. Whenever the Russian peasantry revolted, in the nineteenth century, the Revolution collapsed because it lacked the leadership of a city proletariat; and when in 1905 the workers rose, they did not have the peasants with them.

  Until that time almost all the leaders in all countries had been intellectuals; Marx, Engels, and Lassalle, three German scholars, had provided the spiritual preparation for the Russian Revolution; after them came Lenin, the son of a Czarist official of the minor nobility, and Tchitcherin. It was only with Stalin, Gorky, Kalinin, and their comrades that a born proletariat entered the leadership; but they had much to learn in order to fill the gaps in their education.

  Stalin learned something during the period of his activity in St. Petersburg. The social order was so undermined there that this perpetual fugitive from the police was kept in hiding by a quartermaster of the mounted Imperial Guards. There were periods lasting weeks during which he slept every night in a different house, though by no means always in a bed.

A woman comrade later described his life in St. Petersburg at that time:

"Meetings of factory workers always ended very late since the long work hours made early meetings impossible. Coming out of these meetings Stalin would spend some time in one of the two taverns that kept open until two. He sat there until closing time over a cup of tea. From then until four in the morning, when the cabmen's taverns opened, he walked the streets. He had two dangers to face —risk of being picked up by the police and the raw St. Petersburg climate. In the cabmen's tavern he warmed up over a glass of tea, then dozed till six or seven when he went to the house of a comrade or sympathizer to get some rest."

He himself wrote about the things he had learned in underground St. Petersburg:

"I recall the year 1917 when, after my wanderings from one prison and place of exile to another, I was transferred by the will of the Party to Leningrad. There, in the society of Russian workers, and in contact with Comrade Lenin, the great teacher of the proletarians of all countries, in the midst of the storm of mighty conflicts between the proletariat and the bourgeoisie, in the midst of the imperialist war, I first learned what it meant to be one of the leaders

34

of the great Party of the working class. There, in the society of Russian workers—the liberators of oppressed nationalities and the pioneers of the proletarian struggle in all countries and among all peoples—I received my third revolutionary baptism of fire. There, in Russia, under Lenin's guidance, I mastered the art of revolution."

Lenin, who from his exile abroad not only laid down the theory for the party congresses, but directed internal activities down to the minutest details, sent his newspaper, *Iskra—The Spark*—into Russia, concealed in the covers of cigarette boxes, in the lining of hats, or in capsules dropped into barrels of wine; the periodical was printed in tiny letters on the thinnest paper. It came also to the Caucasus, which, with its anti-Russian sentiments, was primed for a revolution; it was there, and in those days, that young Gorky, who worked on the railroads under his family name of Peshkov, and young Kalinin, a lathe turner, first became acquainted with Stalin, who was even younger than they.

Stalin met Lenin at two congresses. He speaks proudly of a letter which Lenin wrote to a third comrade praising the work of Stalin, and which this comrade forwarded to Stalin in Siberia. In any event, Stalin played no rôle of importance at those congresses, held outside of Russia, in which the young party broke up into Mensheviks and Bolsheviks; as a delegate he made no speeches, and was little noticed by Lenin at the beginning.

He, however, obtained an unforgettable impression of Lenin. "I am nothing but a pupil of Lenin's, and I don't wish to be known as anything else," said Stalin to me twenty years later, and has expressed himself similarly in his speeches.

For a long time Stalin was characterized by his complete self-eclipse behind Lenin. Today Stalin's propaganda puts the two men side by side, and this must obviously be done with Stalin's consent. How the twenty-six-year-old Stalin first met the thirty-six-year-old Lenin at a congress in Finland, was subsequently related by Stalin himself:

"I waited for the eagle of our party, and I expected a big man, one who would tower even physically above the others; yes, I thought of him as a giant. To my astonishment I saw a man of less than medium height, who was in no way to be distinguished from the others. A great man likes to come late to meetings, so that the impatience of the audience is increased; and so that on his entry he may hear on every side: 'Sh! Quiet! Here he is!' But I found Lenin there long before the others; he sat in a corner conversing with a wholly unimportant delegate. This simplicity and modesty, which struck me at once, this desire not to attract attention or to demonstrate superiority, was an outstanding trait in the new chief, and was suited to the simple human masses which were beginning to educate themselves."

During one of their rare encounters, in Vienna, Lenin found pleasure in playing chess with Stalin, in one of the cafés. What a pity that no one photographed the scene! The picture would have been invaluable for the psychologists; the minds of both men were visibly at work, but not with the usual, daily and exhausting tenseness. Men should always be photographed while occupied with their hobbies.

While Stalin's retiring and thoroughly prosaic nature felt itself attracted by Lenin's simplicity, it was alienated, and even repelled, at the same meetings, by the brilliant presence of Trotsky, which had everything that Stalin's lacked. As a matter of fact there is a similarity between the speeches of Lenin and of Stalin in a certain factual dryness common to both. Neither of them made much use of gestures in speaking; in actual life Lenin gesticulated much more rarely than in his official pictures. In physiognomy they were definitely nearer to each other than to Trotsky, with his exciting personality. But Lenin possessed enough devotion to draw closer to himself this enormously gifted coworker, who did not fit in with his own nature, while at this period Stalin must have felt inferior in the presence of Trotsky.

The success of the Russian Revolution, and the failure of the German Revolution, may be partially explained by the fact that in Russia there was, for twenty years, a constant interplay between the exiled leaders and the leaders on the spot, while the German government exiled nobody and imprisoned very few. The more humane methods of the German Empire, which spared its opponents, at least after 1890, resulted in the fact that when the rule of the Kaiser collapsed in 1918 there were no returning exiles, no liberated martyrs, to spread the flames of revolution. This was one of the reasons for the weakness and short-livedness of the Weimar Republic, which let itself be pushed over by

Hitler. As against this, the cruelty of the Czarist regime in Russia was a preparation for the Revolution, both internally and abroad.

Stalin, as a soldier in the army of Lenin, who between 1900 and 1919 transmitted his commands from abroad, and prepared every campaign, acquired importance very slowly during those years; and right up to the Revolution he never once appeared in the foreground. When I asked whether, in his opinion, a revolutionary could prepare himself better at home or abroad, Stalin did not give me a yes-or-no answer, but delivered himself as follows:

"I consider Lenin an exception. Very few of those who were then living and working in Russia were as intimately acquainted with everything that happened as Lenin managed to be, from abroad. I visited him in 1907, 1908, and 1912, and I saw the stacks of letters he received every day from Russia. And yet he himself considered it a great disadvantage that he was never in Russia. The others, those who remained here, rendered great service: for every man that we had abroad there were two hundred working at home. Today we have in our Central Committee, which consists of seventy members, only three or four men who have ever been outside the borders of Russia. But as against this, we have here comrades who have lived twenty years in Berlin, and can't give me a precise answer to a question on German conditions."

Stalin's life in Russia was far grimmer and more dangerous than Lenin's abroad. That was the time, 1905, when the first Russian Revolution collapsed, with nothing to show but a façade parliament, a slight increase in wages, and a slight improvement in the lot of the workers. And even this degree of achievement was due to the defeat in the Russo-Japanese War. At the same time there was an intensification in the persecution of the first Socialists and Bolshevists, though both parties were represented in the parliament by their duly elected delegates, who were able to speak openly and freely for the first time in the history of the country. It was precisely in this period of so-called liberalization, between 1905 and 1909, that the number of political convictions rose from 85,000 to 200,000 per annum. There existed in Russia so-called "Black Hundreds" and "White Fanatics," who wore black masks. The government used violence and illegal measures, exactly like the dictators of our time. It was perfectly natural for the radical groups to retort in kind. In such cases it is very difficult to distinguish between cause and effect. No historian has ever managed to establish who fired the first shot in a revolution. Instead of arguing that it was the blacks or the whites, the angels or the devils, who started the shooting, it would be well to understand that in every instance it is the spirit of history which fires the first shot.

Among the methods of violence invoked by the radicals, there was the obtaining of money for party purposes through robbery. The most famous of these armed robberies was carried out by Stalin himself. On June 26, 1907, there was an outburst of pistol shots and bomb explosions on the main boulevard of Tiflis; men and horses lay dead on the asphalt, and $175,000 of State money had disappeared from the car. The process was called "expropriation," or "ex" for short, and had already been carried out successfully on previous occasions.

Stalin, who was a higher party official, played the same rôle as a general in a battle; he planned and prepared the attack, and had it carried out by eight comrades, two of them women; they belonged, as it happens, to the Social Democratic party. Kamo, the leading figure, and the romantic robber *par excellence,* had only recently lost an eye in a similar but unsuccessful attempt; he was still sick and pale when he led the new attack. The conspirators knew when the new package of ruble notes, to the amount of 250,000 rubles, was to arrive from St. Petersburg at the Tiflis post office, to be taken over by the military in a protected car and transferred to the state bank. A member of the band stood at a corner of the boulevard, and when the car left signaled to the others by opening a newspaper.

Then suddenly bombs flew, soldiers and police fell to the ground on the busy, noonday street. A man sprang forward and threw another bomb among the horses; another, firing a revolver, leaped into the car, seized the package of money, and disappeared. The package was later brought to the office of the director of the local observatory and deposited there; the astronomer, whose mind was on the stars, and not on money, had not the slightest idea of the huge treasure which was lying under his nose.

The attackers left no clue. The wrong people were arrested, and the perpetrators of the attack remained unknown till eleven or twelve years later, when Lenin had the case investigated on the request of a political group. As the numbers of the stolen bank notes had been sent out all over the world, there was a possibility that certain Bolshevists, who had received some of the money for party purposes, and who were still abroad, might be arrested even at this late date.

Lenin jestingly called Kamo "the brigand of the Caucasus," for the latter really does take on the likeness of "the noble robber" whose original type appears in the early ballads of all peoples. When a crime is committed in the service of freedom and justice, the public sense of morality seems to soften with the passage of time; a hundred years after such an incident the poets and balladists are glad to forget the sacrificed victims of their hero, even when he happened to be a murderer. The history of the ancient world is full of such instances.

After a series of fantastic acts of violence, always in the service of the party, this same Kamo was finally arrested and four times condemned to death; in prison, he sent the following note to the inmate of the neighboring cell: "I am quite calm. The grass should be growing six feet high on my grave by now. But I'd like to try my luck again. See if you can find a way of escaping. Who knows if some day we won't have the laugh on our enemies after all. I am in irons. Do what you can; I am ready for everything."

The judges felt so sympathetic toward this fantastic person that they dragged the case out until a jubilee of the imperial family brought with it a general amnesty, and

Kamo was given only twenty years imprisonment. But long before he finished his sentence he was liberated by the revolution and entered on a new life career. We tell this story in order to indicate in what company, and in the midst of what adventures, Stalin passed his youth. Men of this cast have a very different view of human life, having risked their own so often.

Since this story has been suppressed in Stalin's official biography, though it is definitely established that he had the directing hand in the robbery, I asked him about it, expecting that he would deny it in so many words, but that I would be able to get at the truth from the expression on his face.

"In Europe," I said to him, "you are described either as the bloody Czar or as the bandit of Georgia. There are stories about bank robberies and the like which you are said to have organized in your youth for the benefit of the party. I would very much like to know how much of this we can believe."

Stalin began to laugh in that heavy way of his, blinked several times, and stood up, for the first and only time in our three-hour interview. He walked over, with his somewhat dragging footsteps, to the writing desk, and brought me a pamphlet of about thirty pages, his biography—in Russian; but there was nothing in it, of course, about my question.

"You will find all the necessary information in here," he said, and laughed slyly to himself because he had "put one over" on me. The question of the bank robbery was the only one he would not answer—except to the extent that he answered it by passing it over.

His manner of evasion gave me a new insight into his character. He could have denied it; he could have confessed to it; or he could simply have described the whole thing as a legend. But he acted instead like a perfect Asiatic, and even in his smile he looked like a Mongolian. Not long before the Tiflis incident, in 1906, another man who was later to become the leader of a state, namely Pilsudski, had staged a much more violent robbery on a Russian train.

That Stalin was, unlike Trotsky, no born writer is demonstrated by the fact that he did not write his first book—or rather leaflet—till then, at thirty-four. Its chief interest lies in the attempt to solve the problem that has occupied him for a very long time and later led to his great success. The title "Marxism and the National and Colonial Question" is as ponderous and pedantic as Stalin's general style. Here he theoretically grants to each nation that right of self-determination which he reaffirmed twenty years later in his constitution. But here he raises this right to the point where it permits secession and formation of independent states—differing thereby, though only in theory, from Lincoln's conception. In Europe such thoughts were revolutionary at a time when the nationalistic ballyhoo assumed ever greater proportions until this coercion led to war and the dissolution of the Austrian monarchy. Lenin applauded the almost unknown author and wrote to Gorky: "Now we have a splendid Georgian who has gathered and described the whole material."

In June 1913, a year before the outbreak of the World War, Stalin was exiled to Siberia for the sixth time, but now to a frightful region from which a prisoner rarely returned alive. Kuleika, in the Turukhansk region lies twenty miles south of the Arctic circle, a desolate place which consists of three houses and is free from snow only three months in the year. It is the frozen steppe, where a man must live like a northern Robinson Crusoe. There Stalin passed most of the day hunting and fishing, in order to obtain food and to keep himself in motion. Then he chopped wood, to warm himself and the food. He made his own nets and hooks; also the hatchet with which to chop holes in the ice.

A woman in political exile describes the life of these people:

"As a rule only criminals were exiled to the Turukhansk Region; but of late the Tsarist government had begun to send political prisoners there as well with the aim of isolating them from the revolutionary movement. It is not accidental therefore that a group of Bolsheviks and central committee members, Comrades Stalin, Spendarian and Sverdlov, should have been dispatched to Turukhansk. The group was headed by Stalin. From here this group, together with other Bolshevik exiles, maintained contact with Lenin and with the organization within Russia, and with individual comrades active among the workers and in the army.

"All possible means were used. Letters were received from arriving prisoners and sent by prisoners returning from exile. Sailors on the ships, fishermen and even merchants, were used as intermediaries. Letters were carefully coded, and passed through a number of secret addresses before they reached their final destination. At every step there were exhausting difficulties and grave risks. The exiles were scattered over great distances in almost impassable country, and were closely watched. Nevertheless no one flagged and the work went on.

"The village of Monasterskoye in that region was used by the exiles as a meeting place. In addition to illegal visits Stalin was very ingenious in finding legal pretexts for visits to the town. By this means he was able to centralize and regularize the work.

"I recall 1914 and the outbreak of the imperialist war. Stalin took a firm stand against the waverers swayed by propaganda of the patrioteers. He called unhesitatingly for the defeat of the Tsarist autocracy. His prestige among the exiles was such that this firm stand by so trusted a revolutionary was enough to resolve doubts and straighten the waverers.

"The receipt of instructions from Lenin was a great occasion in the life of the exiles. On my way to my place of exile in Turukhansk I stopped at Krasnoyarsk where I received the first text of Lenin's theses on the war. I delivered the material to Comrade Stalin, then at Suren Spendarian's house in Monasterskoye. It is difficult to describe with what feelings of joy Comrade Stalin read Lenin's theses which confirmed his thoughts and were the guarantees of the victory of the revolution. At difficult moments in their underground work the Bolsheviks followed Stalin, having full confidence in the revolutionary intuition of this disciple of Lenin."

What patience, what impatience! There sat these men who had waited and worked twenty years for the eruption of the war. Now it had come and they could not move in their northern solitude! There they sat for almost three years, received little news, often for a long time no newspapers—all this before the age of the radio. Not till March 1917, when the bourgeois revolution broke out, were these exiles, was Stalin as prisoner of the Czar liberated and called back—after four years of forced passivity into the midst of the revolutionary whirlwind!

No government in the world today has been so long in power as that of the Russian Communists. For more than twenty-four years, without a single break, they have been the sole governing power in Russia; and they have not only consolidated their power—they have extended it. Mussolini, with his nineteen years of governmental power, is next to them. In the democracies like England and America, the parties have alternated; ten years has been the maximum duration of a lease of power; in the half-dictatorships even less.

The great experiment of a pure socialistic state in Russia has been only a partial success; but the party which took over the reins in October, 1917, has remained in power. Why have these men succeeded where others have failed? Why are they at the helm after twenty-four years, whereas

Hitler, who has ruled for nine years at this date, will not reach half their record? This question can be answered only if approached dispassionately.

The relatively easy success of the Russian Revolution was due primarily to the backwardness of the country. The highest classes, the imperial family, the court, the upper military and official cliques, were either degenerate or corrupt, and offered no resistance. The middle class, exhausted after a lost war, was intimidated and cowardly. It was the worker who carried out the Revolution which the various working class parties had been preparing for twenty years. The peasants, who at that time constituted eighty-five per cent of the population, were won over when they saw before them the realization of their immemorial dream—the removal of their overlords, the landowners, and the leasing of the land to the peasants by the state. The soldiers, among whom there were no less than 2,000,000 deserters, voted for the party which promised peace.

Thus it was that the two revolutions, that of February 1917 and that of October 1917, were effected practically without bloodshed. It was only later that the tremendous sacrifice of life took place, and that would have been considerably less had it not been for the intervention of the western states.

Were Lenin alive today—and he would be only a couple of years older than Churchill—we might ascribe the long duration of the government to the same causes as have operated in all dictatorships, ancient and modern, from Augustus to Mussolini; we might say that it was due to the interests of the dictator's party friends, or to the fear which he inspired. But in Russia an amazing thing happened; Lenin was able to pass on his power to an heir; and this heir was not a son, but the party of Lenin. It has a record of construction; it presents to the world the spectacle of a new Russia which has not only kept pace in the general upward tendency of our age, but has converted the most primitive and backward country in Europe into the technically most advanced, second perhaps only to Germany.

It is in this heritage of power that we shall find the secret reasons for the duration of a regime which has overcome all difficulties. It overcame them precisely because other men continued that which the founders of the state began. For there is a symbolism in the fact that Lenin died six years after the Revolution, and Trotsky was exiled a few years later, and that these two were in only on the beginning of the reconstruction. The man who did not carry out the Revolution, Stalin, carried out the reconstruction. "After a revolution completely different men come to power," said Trotsky once to me, in his exile; and this historic dictum was a correct one, though Trotsky himself meant the statement ironically.

There is not the slightest doubt that Lenin, the first revolutionary, was also the most important one. Even his rivals recognized him as leader and master, much as Cromwell was accorded the leading position in his day. In contrast to this situation, the French Revolution produced its strongest man last, Napoleon. Stalin, whose personality is without any Napoleonic trait, was nevertheless the man who closed the revolutionary epoch and directed the rebuilding of the country. His enemies accuse him of having betrayed the Revolution, which is definitely unjust. What is certain, however, is that he was not among the great planners of the Revolution; all that can be said of him is that he went along with it, in a capacity of no particular importance. Communism would have come to power exactly as it did without Stalin; but without him its subsequent course would probably have been different.

The men who arrived in Petersburg in February 1917, with the avowed purpose of swinging the bourgeois Revolution leftward, and transforming it into a proletarian Revolution, represented a variety of records, temperaments and ideologies. They hated the bourgeoisie not a whit less than they had hated the Czar. Ever since the institution of the Duma, some eleven or twelve years previous to this date, the Liberal and the Socialist parties in Russia had been at one another's throats; similarly, the political literature of the time is filled with the names and dogmas under which the Socialists fought each other. Two sects belonging to the same church hate each other much more furiously than either of them hates another, outside religion.

A handful of Liberal deputies, princes, lawyers, professors, had taken over the government of Russia, after the collapse occasioned by the military defeat. At the head of the group stood Kerensky. But the young Republic which these men founded attracted no support; it gave neither land to the peasants nor peace to the soldiers. It was utterly determined to beat Germany first, at any cost. Like most Liberals, these men wanted to prove their patriotism, and this was the mistake which ruined them.

For who wanted the continuation of the war, after it had already lasted thirty months? What did the city dweller or the peasant care about Constantinople, the ancient dream of all Czarist power seekers? What did it matter to them whether it was the Cross or the Crescent which floated over the Mosque of St. Sophia. The then hundred and twenty millions of Russia, who felt themselves betrayed, wanted bread and peace, and were profoundly disappointed in the Liberal government.

The one historic act performed by the Liberal government was the liberation of political prisoners and the permission given to political exiles to return. It may be observed generally that Hitler profited immensely from the Communist example, and particularly from Stalin's experiences. When Hitler once asked some of his friends what they thought of Trotsky's memoirs, and all of them expressed the profoundest contempt for this book, written by a Jew, he replied: "For my part, I've learned a great deal from that book."

But earlier he learned from the tolerant methods of the Russian Liberals what he ought not to do.

Kerensky's defeat was due first of all to this tolerance; his policy opened the door for the advancing social revolution.

With the outbreak of the war in 1914 the International had collapsed. In every country the workers were patriotically minded, in every country they felt they were the attacked. Only a handful of fanatical Marxists were passionately hostile to their own governments; a man and a woman in Berlin, four or five political Liberals in Paris, London, and Vienna, who went to prison. What they wanted was the social revolution, which could be brought about only through the military defeat of their own countries.

This conflict exists in every human heart. A feeling for one's own country is an inborn characteristic, just like the feeling for one's parents. But a man easily gives up a war of conquest. Only after a defeat the common man sees through the betrayal, and revolts. This was as true in ancient Athens as it is in modern Paris.

Lenin, who was living as an émigré in Austria, had fled in August, 1914, to Switzerland, and from that center had carried on, with a newspaper, pamphlets, and speeches, against Czarist Russia. He poured scorn on "the Socialists of the Czar" and wanted the defeat of Russia "as the lesser evil."

When, in the spring of 1917, the French and British refused him a transit visa, he got it from the German generals, who hoped by their action to reach an early peace with Russia, and actually did so. But by their action they also brought about the creation of the Communist state.

If Lenin had not arrived in Petersburg, the Revolution of the workers and peasants would never have taken place; all the records prove this, and no one doubts it.

Trotsky, who was at that time not yet a Bolshevik, took a similar view to Lenin's during the early years of the war, though he was less extreme. He was expelled from France, fled to the United States, and was arrested in Halifax while trying to get back to Russia. His twelve-year-old son threw himself with his fists at the English officer who ordered the arrest, but was very friendly toward the sailors who actually carried it out; so thoroughly had he been brought up in the theory of the class struggle. Trotsky was finally set at large. Within a few weeks of each other, Lenin, Trotsky, and Stalin arrived in Petersburg from three different points of the compass.

What did Stalin feel about the situation? For three long years, cut off from all contact with his master, Lenin, he had lived the life of a hunter and fisherman in his Arctic exile. Only once during that period did he have a companion; a comrade stayed with him in his hut for a few weeks, and the two men learned to hate each other cordially, which is nothing surprising when we consider the enforced intimacy and loneliness of their existence.

Stalin came within a hair's breadth of becoming a soldier of His Imperial Majesty, the Czar, and perhaps of being wiped out in the great mass slaughter. The losses of the Russian army were so enormous that even political prisoners were being pressed into service, and twenty of Stalin's comrades in Siberia were enrolled. A defect in his left arm saved Stalin from a like fate. I do not know whether he still suffers from this defect.

It is not impossible that Stalin actually regretted his rejection; for to be cut off from all news of the outside world, and to be condemned to eternal woodchopping and hunting in these days when Russia was fermenting with change, must have brought a man of his fighting temperament to the verge of despair. What his thoughts were during those three years we do not know. Since Stalin was extremely careful, in later years, to have his own and other records and papers sifted so as to leave a favorable picture, his opponents point significantly to the lack of documents relating to that time; for it is certain that he would have published every radical line he wrote. At any rate, we know that on his way back from exile with two comrades, he sent this telegram to Lenin: "Comradely greetings on departure for Petersburg. Stalin."

CHAPTER THREE *Ascent*

Stalin's enemies have vainly tried to create the story of a clash between Lenin and Stalin. In actual fact, Stalin happened to be a blind follower of Lenin and has remained such; but he does not seem to have been a creative element in the Revolution. Lenin, who had sought refuge in Finland for some weeks, seems to have recommended him for election to the Central Committee. For all that, Stalin did not come to the fore, and his name still remained practically unknown to the masses.

The men who, within a few weeks of their arrival, took the Revolution into their hands, and whose names were thenceforward linked together, were Lenin and Trotsky.

Leon Trotsky, one of the most dazzling phenomena of our age, seemed born to supplement Lenin. Lenin chose him as his closest collaborator because he himself lacked what the other possessed: irresistible oratorical gifts, the power of suggestion over the masses, the passionate inclination of a man of spirit for the world of action. Trotsky, who as speaker and writer was far superior to Lenin, had an elastic energy which was not great enough to enable him to direct the Revolution alone, but which was set off and heightened by Lenin's more sober nature. Nor did Zinoviev, Radek, and Bukharin, whom I met in their day of power, have anything like the brilliance of Trotsky, who in this respect has only one rival in the history of Socialism: the German, Lassalle.

Trotsky's rapid rise touched off Stalin's jealousy of this rival, whom nature had endowed with such superior gifts. Character, not principle, created the division between these two important figures, and the division widened and deepened until in the end it was the grim, obstinate, and patient spirit which triumphed over the swift, keen, and brilliant one.

We need only compare the heads of the two men: Trotsky's all forehead and eyes, Stalin's with neither forehead nor eyes. The one slender, the other heavy, the one adroit, the other clumsy. The one physical thing they had in common was their fine hands, which, we may note, are common among dictators.

At every point the men are in contrast: Trotsky is the people's leader, effective externally, Stalin the organizer, effective internally; Trotsky is the polyglot, the citizen of the world, the man of high education; Stalin's training is purely Marxist, his education is limited, he has no knowledge of languages, his contacts have been exclusively with Russian circles. A man of speech side by side with a man of silence; an immensely gifted Jew side by side with a passionate Asiatic.

Both had some of the gifts of their master, Lenin: Trotsky the *élan*, Stalin the endurance; Trotsky as the enthusiast, Stalin as the politician; Trotsky as prophet, Stalin as ruler. We may compare Trotsky to a light, high-speed automobile, which negotiates any kind of road and flies past its goal, and Stalin to a ponderous tractor, which breaks up the hardest soil, turns slowly, and prepares the bed for the seed. If we could imagine a tractor with a soul, would it not look with mistrust and distaste on the graceful little car which overtakes it and is always in the lead?

Just as different was the life of these two men of the same age. Though both had run away from home at seventeen in order to serve the radical movement, their revolt had been caused by dissimilar reasons. Trotsky abandoned the comfortable life of a finely cultured bourgeois home. Stalin wanted to rise from the depth of his father's carpenter shop and told me that the snoopers in the Orthodox school, in which his parents wanted to educate him for the priesthood, had driven him away. At twenty both men had already experienced their first political imprisonments and exiles. Both had been sentenced during the Revolution of 1905, jailed, and had escaped from Siberia, without coming in closer touch with each other.

But the important decade between the middle twenties and the middle thirties which generally decides a man's culture, spirit, and character—coinciding with the time between the two revolutions—they spent under such different circumstances as were prescribed by their nature. Stalin, with the exception of a few weeks' journey through

Germany, never left Russia. He spent his time doing underground work in Russian cities, was again deported, and again escaped back to Russia, came to know neither languages nor nations. In contrast, Trotsky lived for these twelve years in the West, studied Socialism and world politics in France, England, and Switzerland, spoke German, English, and French almost equally well, witnessed the World War for two years in Paris and London, and came, at the beginning of '17, to America. When he wanted to sail from Canada to the Russia of the Revolution, he was arrested aboard by his English allies, carried away on the shoulders of the sailors, interned in a camp together with German prisoners, and not liberated till later.

Stalin lived separated from wife and children. Trotsky, during all his wanderings, lived in greatest harmony with his wife and two sons, one of whom had been born in Vienna.

Enlightened by western science and polemic methods, member of congresses and secret sessions, sometimes allied with Lenin—who was already acknowledged as leader during his emigration—sometimes quarreling with him, Trotsky developed in this time a talent owned by none of his comrades, though all of them were writing: he became a great author, the only one produced by the Revolution, and next to Churchill the best chronicler of his age.

In the meantime Stalin spent his life in Russia as agitator, constantly persecuted and threatened by new imprisonment. It seemed as if Trotsky belonged to the day shift, Stalin to the night shift of life. Was it not inevitable that their characters should develop in two opposed directions?

When Trotsky came to St. Petersburg in the summer of '17, and Lenin had returned from exile, the government fell to these two men in accord with their talent and culture, while Stalin and other fighters had to remain in the background, though they had worked for the Revolution just as long and hard. All the light fell on Trotsky, who, during the negotiations with the Germans in Brest-Litowsk, acquired greater international fame than anybody else, because he became, through his speeches, the spokesman of a new world. Then, when he founded the Red Army during the next three years and led it into battle during its inception, when he stood at the head of all the Russian armies as Minister of War, at the same time guiding the country's politics as Foreign Minister together with Lenin, nobody spoke of Stalin, though he belonged to the Cabinet, too. The world attributed all the victories of the Red Army over the Whites—Koltschak, Denikine, Wrangel—to Trotsky's leadership.

Would not at first innate distrust, then the hate of the less favored turn the man of the night shift against the more and more radiant figure of his comrade? Why had the other spent his life amid the light of western freedom and indulged in the joys of the spirit, while he himself had to keep in hiding? The proletarian cobbler's son was inevitably annoyed by the bourgeois descendance and careful education of his competitor. And had not this man been a Menshevik till a short time ago—that is, less radical than

Stalin and Lenin? What did this son of a bourgeois family know about the workman's and peasant's misery, which he had never endured? Was he better in any way than the sons of the White bourgeoisie who were killed by the thousands? Would he, Stalin, not have been able to direct this army equally well and even much better?

The concussion was inevitable, for Stalin, too, belonged to Lenin's inner circle. Furthermore, Trotsky was induced by his great self-esteem to make fun of Stalin and call him the "Party's most eminent mediocrity."

Stalin was not the only one whose antipathies were awakened by the newly arrived genius. In the eyes of others besides Stalin, Trotsky was the gay child of the world stage, who had been having a good time "out there," while they were laboring grimly in Russia. All Stalin was aware of, was that the whole world was speaking about Trotsky, who was conducting the negotiations with the Germans. When Trotsky, during those days, made his first broadcasts on the new—and nearly the first—world radio station, addressing himself "To All," he emerged for friend and foe alike as the herald of a general peace. Only Wilson made a similar impression, a year later.

What is amazing about the struggle between these two men is that it did not break out over a question of politics, but over a question of strategy. It is impossible not to smile at the picture: a Caucasian cobbler's son, and a Jewish farmer's son, neither of whom had ever been soldiers, both of whom were members of illegal parties, had never had anything to do with war but had been preoccupied exclusively with classes, wages and the Socialist struggle, became field marshals overnight.

Stalin and Trotsky, both men in their forties, now wore uniforms for the first time in their lives. If they knew how to handle a rifle, they had to thank their hunting days in Siberian exile for it. But neither of them had the remotest knowledge of military weapons, of horses, of cannon; they had never given military orders, received military reports; they did not even know how to salute. The most insignificant shavetail was in these respects superior to the two revolutionaries who had passed the war years either in exile or in prison.

Stalin and Trotsky, the two civilians, saw themselves suddenly called to the direction of war which had to be wholly improvised. All at once they were generals, even if they did not have the title; Trotsky was in fact War Minister and Generalissimo combined, even though no formal decision had been taken by the Central Council and the War Council. Trotsky spent the next two years in an armored car, which moved from front to front. Stalin was in command alternately in the Ukraine, in the Donetz Basin, against Poland, and before St. Petersburg.

Formally speaking, Stalin was the subordinate; spiritually he was not less so, during the civil war. But in those chaotic times orders could not be handed out between old party comrades as they would be in a long-established general staff; the result was that fundamentally everything depended on their personal relationship to Lenin. Lenin, too, had never worn a uniform or carried a sword. But Lenin was used to command, for he had been, during a period of nearly twenty years, the recognized head of the Bolshevist group, even though he had operated from abroad.

Since Lenin was passionately devoted to the democratic idea, and even at this juncture declined the rôle of dictator, his moral influence became stronger and stronger, precisely because he appeared to subordinate himself to a committee or soviet. The most famous disciple of Karl Marx was in one respect a living disproof of Marxist theory; he demonstrated to all the other disciples that, though history is indeed set in motion by economic law, its issues are decided by individual characters.

And now they found themselves at the heart of a maelstrom of unsolved problems. They held their sessions at first in the Czarist institution in St. Petersburg, and afterward in the Kremlin, in Moscow. Their task was twofold: they had to lift a land, the greatest in the world, out of the chaos of a shattering defeat; and they had to integrate it into a new social form. They had to defend Russia against the White troops sent against her first by Germany, Poland, and Rumania, and later by England, France, and Japan, ostensibly to crush Communism but actually to secure for themselves provinces and harbors, grain and oil. At the same time they had to hold down their enemies within Russia, and among these were former comrades of other Socialist parties. Under such circumstances victory seemed impossible. The world expected the collapse of the new holders of power to take place in a matter of weeks. They have remained at the helm for a matter of twenty-four years.

Perhaps their triumph may be attributed to the very fact that they were not professionals, but amateurs, that they were not officers trained in a military college, but fighters trained in the school of life. Did not these men, all of them between the ages of thirty-five and fifty, have behind them a youth and manhood filled with struggle? Now faith and necessity alike drove them to transfer their fighting careers from the platform to the field.

The only reading ever done by these three, Lenin, Trotsky, and Stalin, on the subject of war, was the Prussian general, Clausewitz, whose book is still considered a classic. Stalin in particular, having always remained in the country, had studied the corruption of the Russian officer class and the dull obedience of the enslaved soldiers, and had seen in these the symptoms of a social division which was bound to end in catastrophe. It is no accident that during the preceding half century the Russian army had been defeated three times in succession. The question was, who was to blame, the Russian peasant who obeyed orders and let himself be shot, or the Russian officer, who issued orders and was more reluctant to sacrifice himself?

Since the amateurs who now directed the war were convinced that the fault lay with the officer class, and not with any lack of courage on the part of the soldiers, they could not make use of former staff officers of the imperial army, even when these stated under oath that they had long been secret revolutionaries. And yet Lenin and Trotsky had to acknowledge that they could not manage without the advice of the old officers. They therefore accepted the services of a few of these professionals, and always had them watched by tried and trusted party comrades. Trotsky was in the position of a man who does not know how to drive a car, and does not trust his chauffeur, but must sit next to him with a gun and compel him to drive in the right direction. Thus, for two whole years he had to see the revolutionary war being conducted, though not directed, by former officers of the Czar.

Stalin was of another opinion. Since he was one of the few proletarians among the first leaders, it is possible that his hatred of the former ruling class was stronger than that of his comrades of bourgeois origin. Still another factor must be borne in mind; when Lenin gave him his first command at the front, near Tsaritsyn, he discovered a conspiracy among the officers, who were about to turn on the new rulers. Stalin's reports and telegrams are filled with the bitterest contempt for the professionals, who did everything wrong: "What these fellows call the science of war I can only deplore, though I have the highest respect for science as such."

In this summer of '18 Stalin saved Russia and the Revolution.

British and French troops, united with White Russians, had made common cause with Muscovite counterrevolutionaries in order to destroy the Bolsheviks for all time. The stricken land lay in ruins: no railways, no weapons, and above all not enough bread—for the wheat belts of the Ukraine and Siberia had been cut off by the enemy. The only available wheat came from the Volga and the Northern Caucasus, but had to be shipped on this river by way of the town of Tsaritsyn. In that district the small peasants were oppressed by the Kulaks and wheat speculators. Everything depended on the possibility of having Red troops —consisting mostly of badly armed workers with a cap on their head and a gun—transport the wheat into the country's interior. The fate of the Revolution literally hung for several weeks on the defense of this town.

Stalin, arriving there with a few thousand workers, mistrusted the old Czarist officers who were playing a double game or at least under suspicion. But Trotsky, as Minister of War, opposed Stalin's strategy and cabled other orders. Stalin threw them into the wastepaper basket or wrote on top: "To be laid aside." He saved the town, reconstructed this part of the disrupted army, and hindered the enemy from joining his allies in the Ural and on the Volga.

In these struggles the characters of Lenin, Trotsky, Stalin emerge with great clarity.

On larger issues, too, Stalin proved to be in the right as against Lenin and Trotsky. He did not subscribe to their faith in an impending world revolution, and planned the defense of Russia without reference to any such illusory hopes. The following telegram reveals his disagreement with the views of his superior, Lenin: "Believe me, Comrade Lenin, that we are unsparing in our efforts to send you the grain. Had those nitwits, our military experts, not been asleep, our lines would never have been broken." And again, with reference to the struggle with the hostile group of Social-Revolutionaries: "As far as these hysterical people are concerned, you need have no worry. Enemies must be treated as enemies."

On another occasion he formulated conditions to Lenin: he wanted the original plan of operations dropped and his own substituted. "If that is not done, my work on the southern front becomes pointless and criminal. That gives me the right, or rather imposes on me the duty, to go to the devil rather than remain here. Yours, Stalin."

At the same time Lenin was receiving from Trotsky telegrams like this one: "I insist categorically on Stalin's recall." The tone of Lenin's replies reveals his mastery of the art of handling men: he puts Stalin in his place without offending him, and retains Trotsky without dismissing Stalin; he even succeeded in reconciling the two men for the moment. And thus, in the anarchy of a revolution, a superior spirit managed, without issuing military orders, to secure the co-operation of two important men who hated each other.

Similarly as in Tsaritsyn, Stalin threw back the Germans in the Ukraine, liberating Kharkov twice in the years 1918 and 1919. To someone listening today, in the summer of 1942, to the war reports on the radio, the recurrence of the same battles in the same place seems completely dreamlike. Everyone wonders what Stalin must feel as he, now past sixty, is forced to defend the ancient Russian land once more against the eternal aggressor.

It seems that Stalin also contributed to the decisions on the third and fourth fronts in 1919. On the northern front he, in command of the army, hindered the union of Koltschak's troups with the Czechs. When General Judenich, with Finnish and British troops and ships, went against St. Petersburg, Stalin forced him to retreat.

These victories of motley troops with ideals over regular troops without ideals call to mind the first victory achieved by a modern popular army. It was in 1792, when the French revolutionary army vanquished the royal and imperial troops on the Rhine, near Valmy. There it was where Goethe, accompanying the troops as Minister of the Duke of Weimar, spoke the greatest word that anyone belonging to the defeated side has ever thought out or dared to utter in front of his own master. Recognizing already on the evening after the disaster that new ideals could procure victory for weak, untrained troops over a much stronger but worn-out power, he said what Koltschak and Denikin should have repeated after their defeat at the hands of the Soviets: "From this day onward a new era of world history begins, and you can say that you witnessed it!"

But during those days of the civil war, Stalin never had the power which the Central Committee entrusted to Trotsky. Lenin's confidence in a dozen instances gave Trotsky *carte blanche* by a general approval of all orders issued by Trotsky for a given date. Stalin, on the other hand, was always restricted to specific tasks.

Then—as now—Stalin did not shrink from terroristic methods, always defending himself on the ground that this was the only way of saving the Revolution. But in all these excesses he never derived from acts of cruelty the peculiar pleasure which Goering later displayed, when he signed a number of death warrants on the morning of his marriage.

This kind of sadism is always connected with an over-developed joy of living, which betrays the terror of the adventurer at the thought of a sudden and violent end. The hunting lodges, castles, and country villas which afford so much pleasure to a Goering or a Hitler, never entered into the calculations of a Communist leader. While the Nazis, as pictures show us, have adopted the ways of life of one-time royalty, Stalin has continued, down to the present time, to live with severe simplicity.

At a big banquet for foreign guests given by the Academy in the fall of 1925, in Leningrad, I saw the old Bolshevik leader, Kalinin, put aside the two-foot menu and order a Russian fish soup. One result of this simplicity, at any rate, is that none of the old or new Russian leaders ever resembled, as does Goering, an understudy for Falstaff.

In the time of the civil war Stalin lived just as poorly as he had done in his youth and in exile. If his services during the Revolution were slight, they were very considerable in the civil war.

When we go through the records, and read how and where he fought and won in those days, in the Rostov and Donetz basin, we begin to understand the character of his strategy, which he was to employ against the Germans on the same battlefields today, twenty-two years later.

A FAIRY TALE

As Stalin sits today before the same maps, disposing, not of a tiny improvised force, but of a disciplined army, and that the greatest in the world, his life must take on for him the aspect of a fairy tale. He may, in such moments, remember how in the midst of the civil war he suddenly divorced his wife in order to marry the seventeen-year-old daughter of one of his friends. Today she is dead; Trotsky and Lenin are dead; nearly all his comrades are dead. The graying dictator, who learned the art of revolution at eighteen and the art of war at thirty-eight, finds himself today, at the age of sixty-two, perhaps without personal enemies, conducting a world war. When we consider what there is at stake for him, his ideal, his state, his power, and his life, we can better understand the fury with which he and the millions of his countrymen defend themselves so brilliantly against the foreign conqueror.

There are in Stalin's life two bright productive periods and two dark ones. He was powerful and creative in the upbuilding of the Russian industrial state; he is powerful and creative once more in the present life-and-death struggle. But he was only a politician in his struggle with Trotsky, and again during the Moscow Trials. The peculiar elements in his character, which expresses itself in such a variety of reactions and results, are intertwined and interdependent. Goethe compares a man's virtues with the branches which a tree lifts toward the sun while at the same time, and with the same urge, it thrusts its roots into the darkness of the earth, which Goethe compares with the negative side of a man's character.

When Lenin died after six years of power (he was, we must remember, sick during the last two), he left behind him a triumphant party and a pacified country; but the modernization of the state was only in the planning stage. He left behind him a victorious Red army; but it was not a mechanized army. State and army alike could only be created by modern technology. The electrification of the giant country was the first prerequisite for the opening up of its enormous resources, for its defense, and for the social reconstruction. We shall see shortly what Stalin achieved in this direction in the course of a decade.

But whatever he achieved, he could achieve it only by becoming an autocrat.

If we regard this struggle as the prerequisite condition for the iron dictatorship from which the new industrial Russia finally was to emerge, we do not thereby get a more normal picture; but that which at first impressed us as mere hatred and revenge does acquire a world-historic perspective. Looking back today on the first period of the Soviet state, we see only the roots digging into the blackness of the earth; this is Stalin's dark period.

Even for Lenin, whose life was always an affirmation, the latter years were filled with tragic struggles. Like a Gracchus, a Cromwell, or a Danton, he had taken over a shattered social system and a bankrupt state. Every social revolution is confronted by a burnt and desolate field, ruined by planless, conscienceless exploitation, and the soil offers the most obstinate resistance to the efforts of the new farmer. Lenin, like Churchill, began his regime by calling for a period of "blood and tears"; and his voice, like Churchill's, had been raised for a decade and more in warning against the impending disaster. "The dictatorship of the proletariat," he said, "has imposed on this new ruling class an unparalleled burden of sacrifice, suffering, and poverty. Never was the working class in as frightful a condition as today, when it takes over the rulership."

It was not the introduction of Socialism by Lenin which produced this ghastly poverty and want; it was the war lost by the Czar, it was the ensuing civil war, which so disorganized the country that in the year 1922 only 51,000,000 *dessiatine* were sown with crops as against 100,000,000 in 1913. The harvest amounted to 2.8 billion *pud* as against 6 billion in 1913. The production in industry in 1920 was 15 per cent of that in 1913. The World War cost Czarist Russia forty billion dollars; the cost of the civil war was another fifty billion. Lenin had to construct his new state in the midst of a catastrophic collapse, and to sign a peace after a war conducted by the Czar, whereas Hitler could wait fourteen years and take over a Germany which had long been restored to prosperity.

The second tragic element in Lenin's situation was the struggle against his former comrades in arms. Mensheviks, Social Revolutionaries, Anarchists had fought the Czaristic regime with the same fury as the Communists, and they now had the same claim to a share in the government. But the theory and the methods of the reconstruction which was now to follow placed such an abyss between these parties and the Communists that Lenin was compelled, against his own principles, to break up the Constitutional National Assembly and to introduce the dictatorship of his own party. He himself called it oligarchy, and could hardly foresee what would develop later out of this unavoidable resort to force when men of smaller mold would rise to power. That which Lenin did was controlled by his own character, and could not be passed on as a legacy. That a character like Stalin's, with its impulse toward personal dictatorship, should witness this dangerous turn of events and should later seek to perpetuate it for himself was predestined.

For with all his energy, Lenin possessed a natural feeling of friendliness for human beings. He tried to convince his collaborators; Stalin commanded them. Lenin ruled in a spirit of co-operation and consultation; in the building-up of the Soviets, those small but growing people's councils, he saw the emergent instrument of popular government; Stalin dominated the Soviets.

What Lenin valued in Stalin was his knowledge of details and of persons, his working power and the swiftness of his decisions, qualities which only a supreme character would appreciate in a subordinate.

Stalin was an expert on nationalities, and was therefore the head of this department for a period of six years under Lenin; he was thus dealing with one of the two main problems of the revolution. For the Russian peasant and the

Russian worker were not only to be liberated; they were also to achieve independence for their various nationalities. What the world lumped under the name of Russia was not a single nationality; there were some twelve principal peoples and about a hundred related stocks which had been subjected to compulsory Russification by the Romanovs. The country which we today call the U. S. S. R., and which corresponds roughly to the Czarist Empire—this gigantic territory stretching from Poland to Alaska and from the Arctic to the Black Sea—gives every one of its constituent peoples as much liberty in regard to its language as Switzerland gives to each of its twenty-two little cantons. In this respect Russia is actually modeled on Switzerland.

Though he speaks only Georgian and Russian, Stalin is considered an expert on these numerous nationalities; the Ukrainians, Bashkirs, Tatars, White Russians, Armenians, Turkomans, and what not. For all of these peoples Stalin had drawn up, along the line of Lenin's ideas, a sort of Declaration of Independence, in which they were promised the right to control their own destinies and the abrogation of all Russian and Orthodox privileges.

The independence of these peoples was all the more surprising in that the gulf between the educated Russian of Petersburg and the inhabitant of Transcaucasia was a hundred times wider than that between—let us say—a traditional Bostonian and a back-country resident of New Mexico. This brought to an end the stupid struggle of the so-called Russian master class against the many subjugated nationalities; it likewise brought to an end the frequent revolts of the latter against the former. The Russian civil war of 1918-20 was complicated by the intervention of European troops. But these would never have been defeated if the Russian nationalities, which had at last achieved liberation, had not joined the new confederation. In the civil war it was class against class, not race against race. It is for this reason, too, that the Russian peoples are absolutely unable to understand the racial ideas of the Nazis.

When this confederation took shape in 1922, under the name of the Union of Soviet Socialist Republics, its basic principle was the diametric opposite of that of the Nazis: the slogans were help for the troops, money and material to be furnished by the stronger members for the weaker, freedom for every national culture and language. Common to all, as in the United States, were the Congress, the army, foreign policy, and the social basis.

The various peoples did not, however, fall into each other's arms in an outburst of brotherly love. In the Ukraine, in Siberia, in Turkestan there were revolts against the Communist system. Stalin's admiration for mighty Russia contributed to the intensification of these struggles in his native Georgia. The special ambition which we find in the sons of weaker states—and Hitler is another example —provoked Stalin to a furious battle with his former Georgian friends, so that Lenin himself had to come to their defense.

For five long years Stalin nowhere achieved independence. In the war he was officially Trotsky's subordinate; in the state he was one among the nineteen members of the Central Committee, and one among the five members of the Politburo (Political Bureau); in both he was always overshadowed by Lenin and Trotsky. But in one respect he always had a clearer vision than those two leaders. For years both of them believed in the imminence of the world revolution, particularly in Germany. Stalin denied this, and therefore demanded action of Draconian severity in Russia. Long after the triumph of the Bolsheviks, Lenin declared that his own revolution was lost if Russia was to remain the only Socialist country. We may call this error heroic.

But Lenin had one quality which no one shared with him: he confessed his mistakes; and until the end he was never tired of dinning into the ears of his comrades that "we haven't become saints because of the revolution, and we must under no circumstances begin to think of ourselves as infallible." He called a defeat a retreat, and a compromise by its right name; and it was precisely thus that he won the hearts of men to him.

But even Lenin was incapable of avoiding the danger which was entailed in the dictatorship of a party. In excluding from participation in the government all dissident parties, he made the direction of the state identical with the direction of his party. In America, too, the election of a new president, or a change in the Congress majority, means a displacement not only in the highest government positions but in thousands of small ones, which fall to the victor. But the control remains with the Congress, within

74

which the minority party can always address itself to the country. With the Soviets, however, the control was soon limited to the party congresses. For a time the whole country was ruled, in reality, by a couple of dozen men.

Here the third tragic factor, which has always followed historically, came into play. There is this resemblance between revolutions and love marriages: the glory and glamour of the honeymoon is followed by the comparative calm of the common task; the glamour vanishes. The new oligarchy of the Politburo, too, became less and less tolerant, and began to enjoy and to use tyrannically the power which it had reverently regarded as the prerogative of the Idea. On top of this, we must remember, Stalin and Trotsky had become, as army leaders in the civil war, accustomed to issuing military commands. Trotsky had too much to do to be preoccupied with personalities. Stalin learned the trick of transferring unpleasant Soviet leaders to remote posts, and began even in those early years to checkmate his opponents by kicking them upstairs.

The masses were terrified by the dictatorship. Their nervousness heightened by cold and hunger, they rose and demanded free elections to the soviets, freedom of speech, and freedom of the press—in brief, everything that had been promised them. In such circumstances idealists, too, become hard and unjust, and Trotsky shot down those sailors whom he had previously called the pride of the revolution. That is why, in his autobiography, he devotes only two lines to this ghastly incident.

Lenin alone sensed the danger which rose from the resentment of the masses, and made what was almost a complete reversal when he gave up part of his basic principles. He wrote: "Since we cannot take Socialism by storm, we will now study State Capitalism." Like the great strategist he was, he made a temporary withdrawal, and in this he resembled his master, Marx, who in a debate once said, and only half in jest, "I am no Marxist."

The retreat was confined to part of the economy and part of the land, where grain and other commodities were again sold on the open market, and where concessions were distributed, which resulted in the creation of speculators and of a new rich class. Europe declared the revolution a failure. From the dogmatic point of view it was, for today the Russian economy differs little from the war economy of England or Germany.

Stalin began his great career at that time by means of an election the importance of which even Lenin failed to recognize. It really was a Trojan horse within which Stalin, almost unobserved, entered the citadel he was later to conquer. He was elected General Secretary of the Communist Party by the Central Committee. From this post he began to acquire control of all the key positions through which the party kept watch on the entire country. Since he was simultaneously a sort of representative of the Politburo of the GPU and a friend of its boss, Dzerzhinski, he soon accumulated in his hands a vast but practically invisible power.

Thus, in his patient systematic way, he began slowly to

prepare his power. The pressure of hunger and the other results of the civil war made men eager for party jobs. If Lenin was respected and loved, Stalin, precisely because few knew him, was feared like an invisible and harsh god. A General Secretary in this form had never existed before.

The result of this dangerous situation was a growth in party membership so rapid that it had to be cut down by a third. A member of the soviet said at that time, "The English Parliament, as every one knows, can do everything except change a man into a woman. But our Central Committee has even larger powers. It has already made women of the most courageous revolutionaries, and their numbers keep on growing."

Naturally the criticism kept on growing too, and in Lenin's time it dared to be outspoken. Instead of punishing it, Lenin would say openly, "Perhaps our state apparatus is imperfect, but so was the first steam engine. To bring our state machinery up to date we have to do three things: learn, learn, and learn." This was language which the masses understood, and they soon pictured Lenin as the father of his country. That was why a shudder of terror passed through Russia when he suffered a sudden attack. From that day until the day of his death, a period of nearly two years, he was able to make occasional decisions but not to rule.

Lenin had been considered indefatigable. The simplicity with which he lived made people forget that for five years he had not taken a holiday; he had never even relaxed by hunting. Trotsky, whose one recreation was hunting, has explained why Lenin was not a good huntsman. Obviously he was not a great soldier either.

Lenin's genius lay in a swift vision of things embracing a wide range of time: What will be the result of these measures ten years hence if I put my signature to them today? This gift of prevision, or of imagination, which always distinguishes the born first man in a state from the second, was integrated with a character in which modesty and self-assurance were perfectly balanced. Lenin is one of the rare instances in which talent and character help each other along.

Lenin was also the only one in whom no personal weakness cast a shadow on the great passion of his life. A logician, like Karl Marx, his master, he worshiped clarity, numbers, statistics, and hated humanitarian phrases. But two qualities in him gave him the advantage over Marx. The first was capacity for action, which Marx never even had a chance to test. Lenin stands in the same relation to Marx as Marconi does to Hertz: he applied the theory of the mathematician to the practical tasks of the engineer. The second was of a more subtle character. Lenin, the clear, careful thinker, was a Russian through and through; he loved Russia; and in his student days he had known what it was to have an older brother executed for complicity in an attempted assassination. While Karl Marx, with his massive intelligence, wanted to improve the lot of the workers no matter in what country, and was himself an émigré and without a fatherland, Lenin, who was one of the founders of the Third International, could not have been effective anywhere except in Russia, even though he knew the rest of Europe so well. He wanted world revolution, but he triumphed only in Russia, because he knew the soul of the Russian worker, peasant, and official as one knows the garden of one's childhood.

In contrast to this, Stalin admired Russia in his soul, and sought to conquer it. If Lenin was the *born* master, Stalin exerted himself to the utmost to *become* one; and he needed twenty years in order to overcome all his rivals. His self-confidence was thoroughly justified.

Occasionally Lenin's pluck got the upper hand of his sickness, but there were times when he suffered from the knowledge that he could think clearly but could not move and could not speak. He had to calculate from one month to the other whether he would be able to take part in the next Congress or in the next session; he kicked out the doctors who tried to conceal his condition from him, retaining one on whom he could rely for the blunt truth. For months on end he was preoccupied day and night with the question of his successor. The transition from Lenin to Stalin occurred to no one at that time. The only man who, during Lenin's sickness, reckoned on the possibility that his successor would be Stalin, was Stalin.

After a revolution the death of the founder is followed only too easily by anarchy or bureaucracy. At that time Soviet Russia was by no means as consolidated as the essentially older United States at the time of Washington's death. The death of Cromwell resulted, after a brief period of government by his incompetent son, in the collapse of the republic. Lenin understood all this clearly.

During the two-year interregnum the government was actually vested in the Troika, or "Threesome," the Russian name for a three-in-hand sleigh, applied to the three men, Stalin, Zinoviev, and Kamenev, who dominated the Polit-buro and the Central Committee and who were united in increasing enmity toward Trotsky. In the books and the popular songs of the time, in the very folk itself, Trotsky was intimately associated and identified with Lenin. He was also the only one who, in numerous capacities, had soon obtained a complete and penetrating knowledge of the structure of the new state. He had been able in the course of one year to get thousands of crippled locomotives rolling again, and thus to repel the Polish assault. When I looked for him in Moscow in 1925, he was somewhere at the other end of the world, checking up on boots and over-coats for the Russian army.

As Trotsky's moral auspices grew with Lenin's sickness, and he became, without official title, the latter's representa-tive, his tragedy began. The Troika, led by Stalin, got ready to displace and overthrow him after Lenin's death. Trotsky later described how conversations would abruptly cease when he entered the room, and called this the first sign of the conspiracy against him while his power was still in the ascendant. These personal questions constituted at that time the chief substance of Russian politics. The continuity of the new state did depend on the question of the successor to Lenin. In cases of this kind patriotic concern and ambitious desire inevitably go hand in hand.

Lenin's life's work would be endangered if the mutual jealousies of his most capable colleagues were to lead to a break in the party. Men of passionately ambitious character, like Hitler, think more of their power and of their fame than of their work. Lenin thought only of the latter. Chained to his bed, deprived at times of the power of speech, he revolved continuously in his mind the question to which successor he should give the weight of his authority. A year before his death he dictated for the party conference that "note" which was subsequently, and with justice, called his testament. Until his death it was read by no one except his wife, to whom he entrusted it:

"I think that the fundamental factor in the matter of stability is such members of the Central Committee as Stalin and Trotsky. The relation between them constitutes, in my opinion, a big part of the danger of that split the avoidance of which might be promoted by raising the number of members of the Central Committee to 50 or 100.

"Comrade Stalin, having become General Secretary, has concentrated an enormous power in his hands, and I am sure that he always knows how to use that power with sufficient caution. On the other hand, Comrade Trotsky is distinguished not only by his exceptional abilities—personally he is, to be sure, the most able man in the Central

Committee—but also by his too far-reaching self-confidence and a disposition to be too much attracted by the purely administrative side of affairs.

"These two qualities of the two most able leaders of the present Central Committee, quite innocently, would lead to a split. If our party does not take measures to prevent it, a split might arise unexpectedly."

During the very week of the dictation of this note Lenin received a report of Stalin's action against the Georgian leaders. Stalin had directed against his former homeland all the passion of his pro-Russian sentiments, and had deposed the friends of his earliest years from power. Lenin was outraged to learn that Stalin had permitted the use of force in matters regarding which the constitution guaranteed the widest tolerance. Meanwhile Stalin had coarsely rebuked Lenin's wife for keeping her husband too closely informed instead of letting him rest. With these impressions fresh in his mind, Lenin strengthened his "note" by adding to it, ten days later:

"Stalin is too rude, and this fault, entirely supportable in relations among us Communists, becomes insupportable in the office of General Secretary. Therefore I propose to the comrades to find a way to remove Stalin from that position and appoint to it another man who in all respects, except in general superiority, differs from Stalin—namely, a man more patient, more loyal, more polite and more attentive to comrades, less capricious, etc. This circumstance may seem an insignificant trifle, but I think from the point of view of preventing a split and from the point of view of the relation between Stalin and Trotsky which I discussed above, it is not a trifle, or it is such a trifle as may acquire decisive significance."

These two crucial documents were never published in Russia, but their purport varies little in the reports of insiders. The documents themselves were undoubtedly destroyed long ago.

Lenin's anxiety mounted steadily as he lay in his room in the Senate building, definitely aware, from certain indications, that a second attack was due. At this same time Trotsky, too, was confined to his bed by rheumatic pains, and lay in a room in the Czaristic Knights' House. The great courtyard of the Kremlin separated the two men, who exchanged views on the most important matters by means of notes and oral messages transmitted by their secretaries: a truly tragicomic situation.

The new thing about the Troika was a propaganda which had always remained alien to the founder of the state. During Lenin's sickness, and obviously without his knowledge, the town of Tsaritsyn, which Stalin had so brilliantly defended during the civil war, was suddenly rechristened Stalingrad, while another Russian town became Zinovievsk. They had ships, schools, factories named after them. Only Lenin refused to have anything like that done for him, for it was only after his death that Petrograd became Leningrad. Later the cult of personality expanded. At the Paris Exposition of 1937, visitors to the Russian pavilion were confronted in six places by statues and pictures of Stalin.

Unable as I was to reconcile all this with socialistic principles, I decided to ask Stalin himself about it. It had been my experience that dictators, like elephants, became tamer if you teased them.

"I am surprised," I said, "at the hero worship which is more prevalent here than anywhere else. You are the very people who logically ought not to revere any individual. Your materialistic conception of history—which is what separates me personally from you, for I hold that men make history—should prevent leaders from being shown in pictures on the street and from having cities named after them."

This attack Stalin took with excellent poise. He said, "You are mistaken. In Marx you will find that men make history, but not in the way your fancy suggests; rather in their reactions to the definite circumstances in which they find themselves placed. Every generation has a new set of circumstances to face. In general, it can be said that great men are of value only in so far as they are able to deal with the circumstances of their environment. Otherwise they are Don Quixotes. As far as my opinion goes, it is history that makes men. Marx never denied the importance of the rôle of the hero. It is, in fact, very great."

Meanwhile, at that time when the real hero of the Revolution was still alive but was not wholly capable of work, the power of the party machine outgrew even him. Stalin, as General Secretary, appointed his friends as secretaries in the states; they appointed their friends as under-secretaries.

Lenin recognized the danger and dictated an article—his last—to which he gave the title: Better Less but Better. In it he proposed a rejuvenation of the state machine on the basis of greater knowledge and better education.

But by that time the Politburo, with Stalin and his friends, was already so powerful that they did not want the article printed. They dared to suggest that a single number of Pravda might be printed for "the old man," with this article. It was only when Lenin's wife and Trotsky threatened them with exposure that the Troika let the article appear.

Lenin lived long enough to see his state recognized as *de facto* by six foreign governments and as *de jure* by twelve more. He had succeeded in negotiating an alliance with Turkey and an entente with Germany, proving to the rest of the world that the Soviet state was capable of contracting alliances. The growing tension between Japan and the United States, already evident in 1923, resulted in the return of Asiatic Russia to the Soviets. Toward the end of his life Lenin saw peace established on the frontiers of his country, while his party was triumphant within.

He died suddenly in January, 1924. Trotsky, who had gone south for a cure, received the news en route, in Tiflis: Stalin wired him. Trotsky later complained as having been misinformed as to the date of the funeral, so that he might not attend. That Trotsky was unable to hold up the funeral by an absolute fiat shows how far he was already forced into the background.

Thus it came about that Stalin interred the dead Lenin before the assembled people. In a finely phrased farewell oration, he said:

"We Communists are people of a special mold. We are made of a special stuff. We are those who form the army of the great proletarian strategist, the army of Comrade Lenin. There is nothing higher than the honor of belonging to this army. There is nothing higher than the title of member of the Party whose founder and leader is Comrade Lenin. . . . .

"Departing from us, Comrade Lenin adjured us to hold high and guard the purity of the great title of member of the Party. We vow to you, Comrade Lenin, that we will fulfill your behest with honor! . . . .

"Departing from us, Comrade Lenin adjured us to guard the unity of our Party as the apple of our eye. We vow to you, Comrade Lenin, that this behest, too, we will fulfill with honor! . . . .

"Departing from us, Comrade Lenin adjured us to guard and strengthen the dictatorship of the proletariat. We vow to you, Comrade Lenin, that we will spare no effort to fulfill this behest, too, with honor! . . . .

"Departing from us, Comrade Lenin adjured us to strengthen with all our might the alliance of the workers and the peasants. We vow to you, Comrade Lenin, that this behest, too, we will fulfill with honor! . . . .

"Comrade Lenin untiringly urged upon us the necessity of maintaining the voluntary union of the nations of our country, the necessity for fraternal co-operation between them within the framework of the Union of Republics. Departing from us, Comrade Lenin adjured us to consolidate and extend the Union of Republics. We vow to you, Comrade Lenin, that this behest, too, we will fulfill with honor! . . . .

"More than once did Lenin point out to us that the strengthening of the Red Army and the improvement of its condition is one of the most important tasks of our Party. . . . . Let us vow then, comrades, that we will spare no effort to strengthen our Red Army and our Red Navy. . . . ."

This oath Stalin has kept. At Lenin's bier he emerged as the heir, even as Mark Antony did at Caesar's; but, unlike Mark Antony, he was destined to crush the distant Octavian. On that day he was firmly resolved to triumph over all his rivals.

The regal funeral was entirely against Lenin's wishes. But the idea of preserving him as a mummy was the result of an unforeseen circumstance. I learned about it years later, in Switzerland, from the chemist.

"The crowds of pilgrims streaming toward Moscow in January," he told me, "were so large and took so much time that the Central Committee directed me to do something to keep the corpse in a state of preservation for another week. Having succeeded in this operation, it occurred to me to make the corpse completely imperishable. For several months the dead body lay on the table of my laboratory and had to submit to a variety of injections. We began with the leg, so that in case of failure the whole body would not be ruined. It was only after a long lapse of time that we felt sure of the results."

Looking at the dead Lenin in his glass coffin, one is astonished by two things: how small he is, and how yellow he is—that is, his face and his hands. Eighteen years have passed, and he still lies before one unchanged. I wondered what emotions would be stirred by the sight of him thus preserved, in the person who knew him best in life, and I asked whether his wife had ever seen him in the mausoleum.

She had never come there.

CHAPTER FOUR

Rebels Against Rebels

Of all the peoples in the world, the Russians and the Americans are the most talkative. Both flee loneliness, though on different grounds. The American likes to laugh, and when you are alone the best you can do is smile. He likes movement and a common enterprise. The Russians, for their part, get together in order to debate. Among no other people in the world is there so much wordy warfare; this explains the slowness but also the depth of Russian development. Other peoples, too, did a lot of talking before and after their revolutions, and their leaders have left vast tomes of speeches to posterity. But the phenomenon increases a hundred-fold among the Russians, for the simple reason that they possess not just one soviet, or just twenty soviets—*i.e.*, council meetings—but hundreds of them, and thousands of party meetings with endless discussions.

In the four years following the death of Lenin in 1924, very much was said, less done. In Stalin's life this was the period of preparation for his dictatorship. In order to obtain clarification on the new state form, the democratic way of debate was invoked. From the interminable debates of all those soviets, committees, and delegations issued the autocracy of the one man. Napoleon had cut across all debates with his sword; in Russia no one had a sword.

Thus, before the first Russian reconstruction under Lenin and the second under Stalin, four years passed during which no building was done, the time being consumed in great battles of dogmas—in reality the clash of hostile men which took place behind the clashes of principles. Stalin's struggle with Trotsky constitutes the chief substance of those four years. It ended with complete victory for Stalin and the creation of the dictatorship which later enabled him to carry out the reconstruction of Russia.

Just as in Shakespeare's *Julius Caesar,* the struggle flared up at once around the corpse of the leader. During the early weeks it was carried on soundlessly, and was concentrated chiefly between Lenin's widow and Lenin's successor. Krupskaya—this was the name of the earnest woman —had a silent but obstinate battle to fight out with Stalin, for on the question of the publication or nonpublication of those two "notes" which were Lenin's testament on the succession depended Stalin's position for the future.

For thirty years this woman had commanded the respect of friend and foe. Though she had no children to divert her attention and her energies, she had always remained in the background. In the twenty years of Lenin's foreign exile, and in the seven stormy years of his leadership of the government, there were none of those teas, at-homes, and parties which are the favorite hunting grounds of the wives of ambassadors and Cabinet ministers. It must be borne in mind constantly that the first fifteen or twenty years of Soviet life were a gray waste in a gray land.

It was with great tact that Lenin's wife, without being a party delegate—she had, in fact, taken part in the Congresses for years—came openly to the aid of Trotsky at certain critical moments in the ensuing years; and immediately after Lenin's death she wrote him this letter:

"I write to inform you that about a month before his death Vladimir Ilyitch [Lenin] took up your book, and came to a pause over a passage in which you discuss the characteristics of Marx and Lenin. He asked me to read the passage to him again; he listened attentively and then read it again himself.

"And I want to tell you the following, too: the feelings which were awakened in him when you came to us in London from Siberia (1902), underwent no change until the time of his death. I wish you, Leo Davidovich, health and strength, and embrace you.

N. KRUPSKAYA."

This woman demanded in vain that Lenin's testament be read forth in public. Stalin, General Secretary of the party, forced through a secret reading before a Committee, though the Congress happened to be in session at the time. It was four months after Lenin's death that nineteen men got together in a room in the Kremlin and Stalin read aloud the document which was so heavily weighted against himself.

"Nobody uttered a word. It was only when Stalin came to the sentence: 'Trotsky's non-Bolshevist past is no accident,' that Trotsky interrupted and asked: 'What was that?' The sentence was repeated. This was the only word uttered in this solemn moment."

It was thus that Radek, an eyewitness, described the scene to me after he had fallen away from Trotsky for the first time. Trotsky, however, not only contradicted Radek's description against my report, but also denied the existence of Lenin's critical observation regarding him. Since the document itself is no longer in existence, or is inaccessible, the only descriptions obtainable depend on personal sympathies.

Lenin's voice, issuing as it were from behind the glass cover of the coffin in Red Square was capable of deciding not only the succession but, together with it, the political evolution of the country. Both Stalin and Trotsky were praised and criticized in Lenin's testament, but Trotsky was indicated as the more gifted man. However, since it was not an absolute monarch who had decreed the succession, the party Congress could confer the leadership of the state, just as well as of the party, on anyone it considered suitable. There was nothing before the Congress but a moral intimation, but that came from the recognized founder of the new state.

Lenin's mistaken notion that a committee, or for that

matter even a triumvirate, could take over the government of a state which was at once so young and so new in character, derived from his belief that he himself had always governed together with a soviet. Actually he had been dictator, although, to be sure, with the almost uninterrupted agreement of his comrades. Now after his death, there were half a dozen leaders and old comrades who aspired to his position. But there were only two who could be seriously considered, namely Stalin and Trotsky, the first because of the influence which he had so laboriously built up within the party; the second because of the fame he had acquired in the Revolution.

But the deeper grounds for Stalin's triumph over Trotsky must be sought in the epoch itself: The transition from revolution to reconstruction had brought a change in tempo. It would, of course, be wrong to say that Trotsky was nothing more than a revolutionary and Stalin nothing more than a builder; each was both. But the swift explosive temperament of Trotsky showed at its most brilliant in a time of unceasing struggle. Stalin's slow, grim Asiatic nature accorded better with a period on which bitter need imposed the discipline of restraint.

Lenin had foreseen with profound concern that these men could not govern side by side.

Fundamentally Stalin and Trotsky both wanted the same things, namely, to build up the industrial state and to carry on the fight against the rich peasant, the kulak, who had survived in the middle position between the land-owning nobility and the unliberated peasant. But they wanted these things in different tempos, and the tempo was in each case related to the man's temperament. Looking back today on what Stalin later achieved, we are inclined to admit that the spirit of history has vindicated him. It would seem that with his passionate attachment to the Russian nation, which he had made his own, he had come to know its people better. Furthermore, he kept one eye fixed on Asia, the place of his origin, derived thence his standards and his tempo, and did not believe Europeans capable of the social revolution, whereas he already saw this dawning in China.

On this decisive point Stalin proved to be in the right. Trotsky, every inch the western European, had, with all his knowledge of peoples and languages, erred in the matter of Europe's revolutionary tempo. What he called the permanent, meaning the world, revolution came neither in his day nor in ours, at least not in revolutionary forms; in spite of which Stalin did built up this individual state.

Stalin carried out by degrees everything which he had at first fought in Trotsky's political program. In exactly the same way he concluded with Germany the very pact which he had accused his opponents of planning and for which he punished them with the death penalty. Perhaps he was right as far as the element of time was concerned. In this new enterprise which had no historic model to follow, one simply had to govern on the basis of conjecture. This state was overshadowed by a question without an answer: Would the other states, and in particular neighboring Germany, imitate the Russian experiment and facilitate it?

LENIN AND THE MADONNA

When Lenin's testament became public property through having been spread furtively by word of mouth, Stalin submitted his resignation, for he was certain that the Congress, which was his instrument, would refuse it; and that is in fact what happened. He was thus in a position to employ democratic methods in his struggle against the growing opposition led by Trotsky, to base himself on elections and on resolutions accepted by majority vote, and to proceed on these grounds to the reconstruction of Russia. He was in a position to do this; but actually the task was so enormous, so new and so complicated, that in his opinion it could be carried out only by means of commands. This was why he regarded the opposition of the minority as a conspiracy, and resolved that if any man interfered with him, he, Stalin, would deprive that man of his job, his livelihood, his freedom to speak or write, and finally his freedom of person.

To do this was possible only by means of the old Czarist methods—the GPU became so similar to the old imperial secret police that, like the Spanish Inquisition, it justified every illegality in the name of defense of the faith. But in this case "the faith"—the old party program—existed no more as a reality; it had become highly flexible and therefore productive.

Stalin invented, after Lenin's death, "Leninism," and strengthened together with it the cult of Lenin.

I myself have seen the picture of Lenin on the wall of a Volga peasant home opposite the image of the Madonna. Leninism was necessary as a counterpoise to Trotskyism.

But what did the word mean? When Stalin abrogated Lenin's testament, his partisans spoke of an old sick man who toward his end was being fed with misinformation; simultaneously they cited from his earlier works whatever was useful for·their purpose.

The fact that both Lenin and Marx had declared it impossible to institute Socialism in one single country was no proof that it could not now, with the use of much foresight and many detours, be introduced into Russia. The worst of it was that just this struggle and this interminable Russian debating held up the actual process of reconstruction. Stalin felt that he could not rule against the opposition of a strong minority conducted by the most popular man in the country. Trotsky, in turn, felt himself to be Lenin's heir.

But, as against this, Trotsky was totally devoid of the Napoleonic intentions which were ascribed to him. At an earlier time, be it noted, he had never made use of his power as War Minister to commit acts of violence, just as Hitler did in the first months of his power. The fact that Trotsky did not do this was of the essence of his character; he was the man who under all circumstances wanted to submit to the laws of democracy, but he was also the man whose self-confidence filled him with the belief which once filled Danton: "They won't dare to do it!" Far from attempting a *coup d'état,* he even refused to become the official leader of the opposition.

Trotsky, who had first created the army and then led it, now retired from the War Ministry. He took over the direction of the electrical development of the country and the Department of Concessions, and threw himself tempestuously into the new science and the new problems. How was such a powerful, popular, and youthful opponent to be overthrown?

Stalin found two methods: he used printer's ink, and he deprived Trotsky of printer's ink. Almost overnight there began in the state-controlled press a campaign against Trotsky and "Trotskyism." Old letters were dug up and quoted against Trotsky. When he tried to reply, his opponents first delayed the publication of his articles, then changed the text, finally forbade publication altogether. A book in which he drew a picture of the past and future was immediately sold out but was never reprinted. At thousands of meetings and on thousands of posters, in the factories and on the land, they undermined the man's reputation.

Trotsky had not built up any political machine. He had too much faith in the masses because he came not from them but from the bourgeoisie; Stalin, born of the workers, had long studied the technique how to influence them. Thus it was that two years sufficed to ruin Trotsky's name throughout the country, because the millions read all the accusations against him and no defense.

When it became known that Stalin had submitted to the will of the majority of the soviets, there was a universal rush which increased the majority tenfold. The oldest leaders prostrated themselves in order to save themselves, only to perish afterward, deprived of all reputation. Zino-

viev, who also considered himself Lenin's heir, and who
had attracted some attention abroad, at first took up the
fight against Stalin, his colleague in the Troika, hoping to
achieve his overthrow. One of them was stationed in Leningrad, the other in Moscow, and they continued for a long
time to fire their printed shots at each other. Then suddenly Zinoviev made an about-face and submitted, hoping
at least to be permitted to share in the rulership.

How swiftly the pictures of Trotsky disappeared! For
eight or nine years the worker, and often the peasant too,
especially if he had been a soldier, had had Trotsky's picture on the wall. Now when, visiting a friend, he saw a picture of Stalin, he immediately followed the friend's example.

And was it not most natural that these people, wearied
by the struggle of a decade, should want peace, and prefer a
legitimate leader to an eternal oppositionist? They wanted
order and bread, not new experiments.

But the sentiment of the people occasionally broke
through, particularly in the army. At the tenth annual celebration of the Revolution, in October, 1927, Trotsky and
some friends, who came in a car as onlookers, were forced
by the crowd into a blind alley; they were extricated from
the jam by soldiers. Barely had the crowd learned where he
was when it streamed from the official tribunes and forced
Trotsky to mount a stand; the official leaders were deserted,
the celebration was transferred to the persecuted. But
when, a few days later, the opposition started a procession
with placards on which were reproduced, exactly as in

Caesar's Rome, the words, "Read Lenin's testament," the carriers were dispersed by the police. On another occasion a policeman shot at Trotsky's car. Meetings in the open were broken up by the appearance of a couple of hundred automobiles whose continuous tooting made every word inaudible.

In this wise Trotsky and his partisans were constrained to hold illegal meetings. What must their emotions have been when, exactly as in their youth when they had been on the run from the Czar's secret police, they had to flee from their own comrades and find refuge in some pent-up worker's home? Trotsky smiled when, after a lapse of thirty years, he once more saw before him a secret printing press. He laughed when he read in the *Pravda* the accusation that he and Zinoviev were in alliance with White generals. But it rankled, just the same, when his defense was not printed at the Congress.

Stalin knew that Lenin's last words against him were being repeated throughout the country. Instead of repressing them, he was clever enough to repeat them with his own coloring. He said to the Congress:

"Yes, comrades, it is true that I am a gruff sort of fellow. I do not deny it. . . . . I am ready for an open struggle before the Congress. The party will not submit to the will of a single leader. The debates must not be carried too far. Let us not forget that we are a ruling party. Every open expression of disagreement can weaken our influence within the country, and still more abroad. The unity of the party must be maintained. Any man who goes off the deep end will be called to order. The formation of factions within the party will not be permitted; otherwise we shall become fragmentated."

The struggle between the two men deepened as the world political tendency seemed to move in the direction of Socialism and Soviet Russia might have come to the help of other countries. Great Britain's general strike of 1926, which Trotsky foretold correctly right down to the date, seemed to him to be a signal, and he called Stalin to account for holding back: "If we do not intervene directly to support the emerging world revolution, we shall lose the power even in Russia itself."

But what could the masses understand of world revolution or expect from it? During the first years they fought bitterly for the land which they had taken away from the nobility and the landowners, and for their new civic rights. Later they fought passionately for the upbuilding of the industrial state. But in between, during the four years which terminated in 1928, they were without eagerness and without passion, and therefore hostile to every form of opposition. They did indeed notice that their bread had become lighter, and that Russia was now forced to import grain. But they did not want to hear anything more about revolution, or about the English workers to whose assistance they were supposed to rush.

While this mood was on the country Stalin went into action, removed Zinoviev and Kamenev, his two old friends, from their high posts, and finally got the Congress also to remove Trotsky from the Politburo.

Now Trotsky took up the struggle, and on excellent grounds. Chiang Kai-shek, who had made an alliance with the Communists, suddenly made an about-face and carried out a bloody purge. Stalin seemed compromised, for it was he, the Asiatic, who had strengthened the bonds of friendship with the Chinese leader and had recommended the creation of a great Asiatic block of 600,000,000 against the British Empire. Now Trotsky accused Stalin of betraying the world revolution, and eighty-three well-known leaders added their names to the manifesto.

In this dangerous situation Stalin risked everything, and actually carried out his *coup d'état*. He had the subservient Congress Committee pass the resolution sending the leader into exile. Certain passages in the fiery debate have come through to us:

STALIN: You, Comrade Trotsky, cannot even summon the courage to defend your own formula.

TROTSKY: A slogan which some one else invented. I have nothing to do with your slanders.

STALIN: Comrade Trotsky knows very well that I can prove everything with documents.

TROTSKY: You can prove nothing. You are a liar!

STALIN: I leave the big words to you! I will submit the papers of our comrade for examination.

Within a few days the Congress resolved to exile Trotsky. He refused to accept the sentence. When the police came for him he remained sitting, so that the men had to lift him in their arms and carry him down the stairs by force. His sixteen-year-old son slipped out between them and called down: "Comrades, they are carrying Trotsky away!" At the station the crowd barred access to the platform. Trotsky was carried back to his house. There was a delay. The next day there was a new maneuver; the train started from another station. For seventeen days Trotsky, his wife, and his son traveled to the Kirghiz country, into the Siberian exile out of which he had escaped twenty-one years before, at the same time and by the same means as Stalin. At the villages on the way the son foraged for bread, butter, and writing materials.

It was then that Trotsky showed that he could rise superior to destiny. In this tragic situation he was able to crack jokes, to put together the shattered hearth of their little home as an enterprise in "reconstruction," to appoint his son "Postmaster General." At the end of the world, in the midst of malaria and wild dogs, they installed themselves with classic humor. Trotsky plunged into the geography, history, and economics of Asia. A picture shows the three of them with a borzoi, the mother resting her hand lightly on her son's shoulder and looking up with the utmost trust at her husband: the idealist's family.

It was not for nothing that these people had been exiled and held prisoners in their youth. They knew all the devious ways by which a government can be deceived. But so did Stalin, who now had to play the government's part; he knew them only too well. He recognized the fact that the 3,000 miles between Trotsky and Moscow were not enough.

The enemy had to be gotten out of the country. One year after the exile a decree of the secret police was read to Trotsky: having plotted to take up arms against the Soviet Union, he was to be deported to Turkey.

After all the hardships of a sleigh journey through mountain passes in January, after a journey of 4,000 miles which took twenty days, they reached the Black Sea. The steamer was frozen in and had to be freed by an icebreaker so that it could carry the three deportees to Constantinople.

At the same moment Stalin, frozen in the Kremlin, also felt himself freed as if by an icebreaker. The enemy was gone. Now he could take up the work of reconstruction. But as he turned his back on this interlude, he happened to catch sight, in the last report handed him, of the name of the ship on which he was having Trotsky taken out of Russia.

It was the *Lenin!*

When Trotsky was gone, Trotskyism still lived on. Millions loved him, and a number of important leaders secretly stuck to his ideas. This might lead to plots that also might be called counterrevolutions. We cannot here analyze the nature of this opposition.

Stalin, who was just beginning his work of reconstruction, must necessarily give half of his forces to the fight against Trotskyism. At the end of 1934 the assassination of his comrade Khirov took place in Leningrad. All Russia felt that the shot had been aimed at Stalin.

Now he took the offensive: in two, really three, monster

trials he advanced against his enemies, and in the end annihilated Trotsky in executing his followers.

That Trotsky himself was incorruptible in his methods
is proved by his entire life. But in the embitterment of the
last decade or so, he sometimes permitted his policy to be
based on Stalin's attitude, and perhaps advocated certain
measures because Stalin had rejected them. On the other
hand he had, in the last year of his life, 1940, overcome all
feeling of revenge, and wrote in support of Russia in the
Russo-Finnish war, which had, after all, been started by
Stalin.

Among the fifty or so Bolshevik leaders whom Stalin had
condemned in the three great trials as Fifth Columnists
there must have been at least a few who did not recognize
their own motives, as is frequently the case with idealists.
No one dared make the suggestion of private advantage as
motive.

Three of them I had met. These men may well have
believed that by a pact with Germany, at that time still
enormously superior, they could avert the danger of a
military defeat. Their opponents called this high treason.
But what is high treason in revolutionary times? Where do
the boundaries stop? Did not Lenin sign a peace with the
same Germany early in 1918, and was it not only the subsequent collapse of Germany which saved him from the
ghastly consequences of a mistake which every rival of his
could otherwise have called high treason?

The most staggering feature of the trials were the confessions made by all the accused. There was even talk of

poison and hypnotism, to which the manly and healthy bearing of the deponents was enough to give the lie. In many countries confession constitutes proof, as, for instance, according to the American Constitution (Article 3, Section 3). In Soviet Russia the fanaticism for the party goes to the point that you have to confess everything the party orders. It should be noted, however, that the right to make a statement was accorded to those only of the accused who had already confessed in secret proceedings. But it is precisely this technique of accusation, so suitable for a falsification of the entire picture, which speaks for the veracity of the confessions.

Or who would seriously believe that men who had once so courageously maintained their views in the teeth of all the threats of Czarist courts would now suddenly dissemble when the whole country was listening to them? These accused men were the comrades of that Spiridonova whom young Czarist officers tortured in prison by applying lighted cigarettes to her flesh, in order to make her reveal the names of fellow revolutionaries. She felt her skin burning and remained silent.

In all probability most of the accused were just as honest in their motives as Stalin was in his. Here, too, personal and objective motives were closely intertwined. Perhaps Stalin was as little conscious of his feeling of revenge against Trotsky as the latter, together with his friends, was of his hatred of Stalin. Both parties wanted, at all costs, to save the young state for the founding of which they fought all their lives. In such cases the question of right disappears, and power alone decides the issue. Had Stalin, at that time, been overthrown by his opponents and condemned to death, which might very well have happened, he could today appear in the same rôle of martyr. Had his opponents triumphed and then signed a pact with Germany, they would in all probability have been attacked by Germany, during the Second World War, in exactly the same way. The fact that they were the ones to be shot, while Stalin today lives, rules, and struggles, raises one of those questions of power which we settle, according to our opinions, by talking of chances or of the genius of the victor.

It is best to regard such an event as a drama. The higher reality of tragedy lifts us above the accidents of time and circumstances. What happened during the Moscow trials had already been poetically expressed by Shakespeare, Hugo, and Schiller. Revolution ever devours its own children: and this with deeply philosophic reason, because the feelings of love and hate always dwell close to each other. The passionate glance and tone, with which I heard Trotsky speak of Stalin, Stalin of Trotsky, were certainly not the only ones thrown by both at each other. Is not a struggle tragic in which both adversaries are right and in certain moments even convinced of their enemy's righteousness?

The records of the Moscow trials represent a human document of first rank and will one day, transformed by an impartial poet, arouse posterity, just as we are moved on the stage by Savonarola, Cromwell, or Danton. Here a wielder of power had discovered that those planning to kill him and his system were not the arch enemies of his world, but the oldest friends with whose help he had founded this new world. The struggle for power merged here, as everywhere in history, with the struggle for principles. Was not socialized society the common aim of Trotsky and Stalin? Did Trotsky and his followers want to become Fascists in order to rule? Only he who has never looked a genuine revolutionary in the eye can even consider such a perversion.

The most important disclosures in this story were made by Radek, whose confession and defense, together with his mastery of dialectics, alertness, and acumen, were sufficient to make these trials immortal. Any admirer of the spirit, recognizing in this force—and not in power or numbers—the master of the world, will be grateful for the fact that Radek saved his life through his confession and may perhaps be today, after five years of prison, close to his liberation—in case he is still alive. With his presentation and self-analysis he has clarified the procedure for all times. We have seen that out of a whole epoch nothing may be preserved from the dust of libraries and passed to posterity except an anecdote, the answer, the glance, the gesture of a defendant.

It is true that Radek—and with him the others who behaved in similar fashion—was not guiltless just because he continuously pleaded guilty in his destructive manner, "even in regard to intrigues of which I was ignorant." Actually he was guilty within the framework of this social order; for he wanted to destroy it and took steps to fight, together with the arch enemy, against his own comrades and superiors.

The uncertainty felt still today about these trials is not caused by the things which were concealed, but by those evidently added under the suggestion of the procedure. For the strongest proofs were not needed against the accused men sitting in court, but against the man sitting 8,000 miles away in Mexico: against Trotsky, who had to be defamed before the Russian people at any cost. Therefore, when Radek spoke of Trotsky's letters—the chief proofs of the conspiracy—this experienced politician might well have quoted as much of their meaning and content as could be useful for the political situation and his own salvation: after all, the letters were not there any more. Perhaps nothing could have been more ingenious than to exaggerate Trotsky's written instructions and his conversations with another defendant in such a way that he appeared as arch traitor to the listening millions, while Radek and his friends seemed to be penitent sinners.

I heard Radek speak about Trotsky in Moscow in 1925 and 1931, before and after his first defection. The first time, in his small lodgings in the servants' quarters of the Kremlin, he spoke to me enthusiastically of the other who was then away on an official journey. Later he declared with a tone and mien that seemed to me somewhat too solemn, almost clerical, that he had searched his heart during his exile, re-examined everything and recognized the absurdity of Trotsky's program. If Radek, according to his confessions before the court, drew closer again to Trotsky soon afterward, and finally, as his representative, steered toward treason by intending to let the Germans enter the country, this is motivated by no personal whims, but by fluctuations common to politics and discovered hundreds of times in private historical documents.

Schiller has said a daring and dangerous word about conspiracies: "If it succeeds, prompt pardon is its lot." In this sense the Moscow defendants were guilty only because they were not successful. Every treason, once accomplished, becomes legitimate, making lawful what had been unlawful just before. The same is true in war. The criminal who has killed his rival and been imprisoned by the state for life, may, in the face of threatening defeat, be pardoned by the same state and sent out as soldier under orders to mitigate his first crime by killing the country's enemy.

Radek, constantly urged by the prosecutor to confess his treason, could not be enticed to deviate from his clarity. "It is a different matter," he declared, "whether one sees in war a possibility to create conditions under which one may realize one's ideas, or whether, setting the whole political significance aside, one aspires to fight against one's own country in order to gain power. It is always possible that war may break out at this moment, be lost, and sweep all of us away."

These arguments are as typically Russian as the passionate interest taken by hundreds of millions in these proceedings, which they followed for days on the radio. It is only possible to understand these accused men with their passionate self-accusations by thinking of Dostoevski; and we are amazed that the Russian character has remained the same in the midst of such an active period, has not been changed by this great movement. Such trials are possible in no other country; for nowhere, not even in France, would the judges have patience and interest for such subtle shadings in the souls of men whom they might sentence the next day to be executed as conspirators.

Also Stalin is too much of a Slav to have followed the proceedings against his arch enemies with as obtuse and brutal a mien as that displayed by Goering at the Leipzig trial after the Reichstag fire of 1933, when he turned his brutish face and barking voice against the accused Dimitrov. This deep participation in the inner life permeating leaders and followers in Russia has decisive practical consequences. Without it the Russian army, which means the people, could not persist against the soulless German troups. In the last analysis wars are not decided by the number of tanks, but by the depth of the people's feeling. The Russian soldier defends passionately what he has just acquired, while the German coldly conquers the object that he has been ordered to seize. In the end he will be defeated.

Fundamentally Stalin's idea about the future of the Soviets differed only in one point—but this a decisive one —from that of his enemies: both parties foresaw the German attack, but Stalin believed in victory, Trotsky and his followers in defeat. Stalin evaluated the Russian and German forces in the right, the others in the wrong way. In 1937 he ordered that thirteen of his former comrades should be shot because they had sought that alliance with Germany which he himself concluded two years later, though in a different form. As none of the accused men were under suspicion of having committed treason for the sake of personal advantages, the motives of the two parties are the same, and only their belief is at variance. But it will be found that a leader has always more faith in his cause than a follower who would like to be in the former's place and go him one better. The powerless rival can best maintain his self-esteem by criticizing the more fortunate competitor. If both are philosophers, or the times are calm, the successful man may smile and pass on. But in times of stress and danger the other one must be destroyed.

Stalin combined Asiatic methods with Russian psychology. Also Trotsky, though more of a philosopher, did not recoil from terrorism. Trotsky, had he been in Stalin's place, would have concluded the pact with the Germans, foreseeing that one of the parties would break it. Trotsky, too, would have expanded the army, which he had first founded, in the same imposing manner and led it with the same *élan* against the Germans.

CHAPTER FIVE *The Colonizer*

Joseph Stalin is a pioneer; he is the greatest colonizer of our age. If we compare results and not methods, he comes closest to the great pioneers of America.

But for the Russians it was both easier and more difficult. It was easier because to America came men and women from foreign lands; they began to clear the primeval forest, to open up the unused stores of metal, to unlock the wealth of natural resources. Every pioneer was a miniature discoverer. As against this, Stalin and the Russians had almost nothing to discover. They had before them a land which had been studied for centuries, a land which had remained backward and undeveloped only because of an antiquated social order and because of the laziness and arrogance of a small ruling class.

On the other hand it was more difficult for the Russians because their struggle with the former possessors—their civil war—was costlier than the struggle of the Americans with the Indians. For three years a war was waged against them from the outside, and for another ten years they lived under the threat of war, and all this while they were in the midst of a new system, subject to continuous experimentation and change. What is taking place today in Russia is the self-defense of pioneers, twenty years after their first conquest, whereas America had almost a hundred years in which to develop peacefully before the two wars came. Hence the feverishness, the rapid tempo in which the Russians had to develop their country. Modern technology did not demand this tempo; it only made it easier.

Why is it, in spite of all this, that history does not hold up any one name as the leader, the directing genius, of the American pioneers before the year 1770? The answer is, because in America everything depended on the individual, and communities arose only when a new area had been cleared and built up. The legends and songs and pictures of America refer, with few exceptions, to the unknown pioneer, and not to any one man who thought everything out in advance.

There is no central idea-man of colonization. Time, locality, and circumstances demanded and permitted only a slow impersonal development. That age, which did not know the word collectivism, developed one of the two richest countries in the world, collectively, voluntarily, without commands and without plan.

In the other of the two richest countries the national wealth developed under the dictatorship of a class which was simultaneous with the dictatorship of a single man. Hence the paradox that in Russia, where 180,000,000 human beings seem to govern themselves and to enjoy every kind of freedom, it was in reality a small group of men who worked out a plan and spread it like a great net over the country. The natural resources of America were opened up in complete freedom for the individual; those of Russia in the complete absence of such freedom. America grew like a tree; Russia was constructed like a machine, and has an engineer who designed the machine.

Obviously he neither invented nor built it all by himself. In conversation with me Stalin specifically relinquished any claim to have been the discoverer of Russian reconstruction. But a people which had only just awakened, and at the very moment of its awakening had been given a rude shock, had to get itself an idol, a demigod, particularly since God had been deleted from the picture. Since this man was able to unite all the power in himself, it was possible to canalize the reverence of the entire people toward a single name.

In reality Stalin inherited his plan from Lenin. If his propaganda machine denies it, he does not. Lenin called for a fifteen-year plan for the electrification of Soviet Russia, and had the plan drawn up. This was the groundwork, and Lenin formulated the famous phrase: "Communism is the Soviet State plus electrification." And actually it took fifteen years to carry out the plan, but in enormously expanded form.

You ask: who has accomplished this great work, who has awakened the sixth part of humanity and changed the world's most backward people into the most modern? Call this fateful question in the forest and wait for the answer! A single word will be the echo: Need! Not the dogmatic will of a few dreamers or followers who wanted to realize the doctrine of their prophet, not Marx and Lenin, who were presented to the bourgeois world for so long as stubborn fanatics, were the fathers of the Russian revival. Need and danger saved this part of the world, while shaking it to the very depth. This consideration alone should teach the frightened old world that the same thing will never be repeated in flourishing countries. But, if the convinced Socialist hopes today that the growing impoverishment of the lower classes will enforce such a transference of social justice, he makes a virtue of necessity.

Hunger and war, the danger of renewed hunger and war, forced the Soviet Union in its beginning to transfer the planning of the entire economic system to an all-powerful state. It was the famine of 1919 and 1920 that compelled the new Soviet government to take up the battle against the rich peasants (kulaks) who wanted to withhold their wheat and dreamed in the midst of the disaster of "business as usual." Thus four thousand state farms and fifteen thousand collective farms were forcibly founded in the first three years, while the harvest was increased from two to five million tons. But this was only a stammering beginning without a broad program.

These are the quick deeds and swoops of a desperate leader who wanted to overcome the country's first vital crisis at any cost. Lenin resembled a physician trying to save a new-born, almost dying child by violent means—at the risk that these means might kill it. If he succeeds, the mother worships him as a savior; if he fails, he is accused of murder. The whole bourgeois world hoped that the child might die.

But after the worst was over, the threatening elements of hunger and war were replaced by the systematic plans of powerful intellects. Will took the place of fate, method that of chaos. Then Lenin became the leading head of a reformation which today, twenty years later, seems exemplary to millions of workingmen in foreign countries. This little man with the bald Slavic skull, firm jaws, cunning and kind eyes; this unknown thinker and fighter who had just returned to Russia simply resolved to make a wideawake industrial and agrarian state out of the sleeping agrarian state.

His master, Marx, had written that Socialism would be founded on electricity: a magnificent anticipation by Marx at a time when electric power was in its inception. Lenin called the whole undertaking electrification. In this case we can even watch him think. In 1920 he wrote the following to a comrade in a private letter:

"Couldn't you work out a plan—not technical but political—which the proletariat would understand? Maybe in ten years (or in five) we shall build 20 (or 30 or 50?) power stations which would cover the whole country with a network of stations, each with a radius of let's say 400 Werst (or 200 if that's all we can get). We need such a plan to show the masses a project that's easily understood and for which they can work. And in ten (or twenty) years we'll have electrified Russia, all of it, industry and agriculture." How valuable is such a letter! Is it not as beautiful as Michelangelo's first sketch for the dome of St. Peter's? Simplicity, improvisation, daring design, demands of grandest proportion! This master, too, has not seen the completion of the dome.

Soon afterward Lenin called together about a thousand men, experts of all countries for all substances and metals, mineral deposits, machines, wheat, domestic animals. He collected geologists, electricians, technicians, hydrologists, chemists, physicists, physicians, industrialists, teachers, sociologists and asked them three questions: How rich is the Soviet Union—including Europe and Asia—in raw materials, water power, native flora and fauna? Where should new industries be constructed and how distributed? How could the proletarian, the unschooled workingman and peasant, be educated for technical work? He expected to get the answer within three months.

The experts needed ten, but even this first design contains intangible magic. It represents, like the calculation of a still invisible planet, the most beautiful instant of a great moment. Already then the whole people were urged to participate in the work. Everyone had to give out information. Never has a scientific undertaking been managed in such a popular way. Finally this body presented the country with a book, a *Plan of Electrification,* containing all the answers.

"I've just finished the book," Stalin wrote to Lenin, praising the plan. He immediately added a slur on Trotsky, who had worked out a different plan. "Trotsky is an artisan from the Middle Ages who thinks he is an Ibsen-hero and has received the call from an old legend to save

Russia." After this malice—also stylistically interesting—he proposed to Lenin: "1. To lose not a minute by further debating. 2. To begin at once with the practical execution. 3. To devote one-third of our labor to this work, the other part to the current needs. 4. To call practical men who know how to work with definite figures. 5. To enforce propaganda of the press. 6. To let all the former plans disappear." Systematic, energetic, without pathos, in the typical Stalin manner. That he wants to serve the present and future in the ratio two to one is almost paramount to a prescription for young reformers.

But suddenly everything was over: immediately after the design had been finished, the uprising in Kronstadt broke out. The foreign powers of the West threatened the country again: the world revolution—especially the one in Germany—expected within a few months, failed to materialize. Lenin made short work of the new situation, accomplishing what might be called his masterpiece: He allied himself for the time of transition with his enemy, capitalism, and introduced the so-called "NEP." The old world ridiculed the new one. It seemed as if the whole magic had evaporated into thin air.

When Stalin, after overcoming Trotsky, practically became dictator, the first thing he did was to combine Trotsky's plan with that of Lenin. He called this the "Five Year Plan." What Lenin had demanded in 1920 speaking in the Moscow Opera, and what the West had pushed aside with the jesting word "Electro-Vision," was inaugurated in 1928 by Lenin's pupil and successor, Stalin. The precious eight years between the two dates had to be sacrificed to the battles against the invading old world, then against the old powers in the new world—the rich peasants—and at the same time to the struggle between the party leaders. The one-third of his labor that Stalin wanted to devote to the future did not become available till he alone was the ruler. Thus the greatest technical undertaking of our epoch has actually been begun and finished under the terrorism of a dictatorship.

Therefore to Stalin belongs the credit for having in the course of a decade lifted the largest country in the world, and the richest in natural resources, from a backward peasant state to an industrial state, and for having at the same time transformed its agriculture by American methods and carried culture, education, science, and, above all, the possibility of obtaining these, literally into every one of its cottages. That Stalin should have done this on a Socialist basis is due to no discovery of his, or of Lenin's, or of Marx's; it only happens to be the sharpest manifestation of a natural development which may be observed in all countries in various tempos and in various forms.

The nice distinctions between Socialism and Communism, which have today become a parlor game for scholars and politicians, have always had their counterparts whenever the world has shifted in the direction of radicalism. When circumstances make compulsory a change in a bank, a stock company, or a national constitution, the older people are always less afraid of facts than of names. Twenty years ago somebody started the grandmother's fable that

Socialism means the common ownership by all of all things—women included, wherever possible—and that under a Socialist regime every idiot and every loafer would earn as much as a gifted and industrious person. As a result we today find people in favor of nationalization of public utilities but shying away from a word one-half of which—as far as its real content is concerned—has been adopted by all the warring states. While Lenin's "War Communism" has long since been modified into a state with Socialist principles, the war has stepped up the national economic management of the democracies. The two developments are converging. There is no such thing today as a planless economy.

Neither Stalin nor Lenin are the inventors of planned economy. Two Germans have invented it, just as two other Germans, Marx and Engels, had first evolved the theory in general. Both pairs contained one Gentile and one Jew. All four of them, considered as lunatics or criminals by official Germany between 1870 and 1910, were laughed at, exiled, sentenced. Generally known is the story of the two German emigrants, Marx and Engels, and how they shouted, from English soil, their world historic prognostication into empty space, as it were. They were, like their two successors, pupils of the German philosopher, Hegel, who may be called the most modern philosopher today, more than a hundred years after his time. He influenced the statesmen of the twentieth century as Machia-

velli those of the sixteenth. As he defied the state and worshiped power, he is quoted by Mussolini on one, by Stalin
on the other side with reverence.

Ballod is less well known. He was a professor, allowed
to lecture on economics at the University of Berlin, but
generally ignored. A strange, stubborn, independent man
—formerly a priest and geographer—he had written his
book, *The State of the Future,* in 1898. As almost nobody
read it, and the few readers let it pass on account of its
Prussian attitude, smiles instead of punishment fell to his
lot. But there lived an unknown Russian emigrant, Lenin,
who knew German very well: this man was fascinated by
the book, had it printed in Russia in 1906, and reprinted
many times after the revolution. For here everything that
Marx and Lenin wanted to use for building a new society
was demanded in a rational way for the good of the state,
but according to a strictly national viewpoint, with Prussian obedience and command: all the means of production
and foreign trade were to be taken over by this state of the
future, while economic life and every kind of labor were to
be regulated from above.

When Lenin conceived the plan in 1921 to electrify
Russia, he wrote that one should only look toward Germany: "There Ballod has proposed the same thing, but it
remained the dream of a single man. We have given this
thought over to the state, called in hundreds of specialists,
and received an economic plan on a scientific foundation
within ten months." Ballod, too much of a German even to

wish for the realization of his dreams, lived to see Lenin, but made no move, because the world considered the Bolsheviks as incarnate devils.

In the meantime another citizen of Berlin had, just before the world war, given an outline of the same idea, but in a lucid and seductive style. This was Walter Rathenau, an extremely gifted Jew. When, later on, the Weimar Republic appointed him to the position of Minister for Foreign Affairs, he was a lost man, for even before Hitler the Germans would not tolerate a Jew in a leading position. The Nazis assassinated Rathenau, and subsequently Hitler had a monument put up to the assassins on the spot where they committed suicide while fleeing arrest. Other participants in the crime who escaped later were promoted to the highest ranks by their gangster leader. Walter Rathenau was one of the inventors of the planned economy which since his time has been adopted by all dictators and by all democratic countries. It is being applied in a variety of forms in the five or eight capitals of the world. After the war, every nation will choose its own social forms in keeping with its character and history, but none will be able to turn back to a completely private economy.

The Socialist state was able to become the most modern of all countries precisely because it had been the most backward. In the little Swiss village in which I have passed most of my life the electric light came immediately after the oil lamp; gas lighting was skipped. Russia, too, skipped the gas-light period, as it were.

Stalin forced the transformation of Russia in exactly the same way as Peter the Great had done. When I therefore asked him whether he did not feel himself to be the successor of the latter, he denied it peremptorily:

"These historic parallels are always dangerous. But, if you insist on it, I can only say the following: Peter"—he purposely omitted "the Great"—"only brought one stone to the temple; Lenin built it. But I am only Lenin's disciple, and my only desire is to be known as his worthy successor."

When a dictator strikes such a pose of humility, you may be sure that something is wrong. That this verdict of Stalin's was both false objectively and disingenuous personally was later proved when he had the movie film Peter the Great released: the scale and style were on such magnificent lines that the parallel was inescapable. Peter called the people a malleable mass. In this respect he, like Stalin, resembled Pericles, who was also a spurious democrat, being in reality an autocrat.

Stalin might even have derived some advantage by pointing to the specific difference between Peter's colonizing mission and his own. Both began as dictators. But in the course of the years a new factor emerged. While the peasants fought the new reconstruction, the rich ones furiously, the poor ones passively, there arose among the workers, and particularly among the youth, a genuine enthusiasm; and this alone could crown Stalin's work with such brilliant results. When the Five Year Plan had been under way for two years, the workers in most factories undertook to put it through in four. They actually managed to complete 93.7 per cent of it in four and a quarter years.

When opponents speak of propaganda, it is proper to ask what national movement has ever been carried out without propaganda. Pericles manipulated his voters, the harbor workers, for his annual re-election with the same skill as Caesar. Stalin had a much more difficult job, for the land was not yet developed. When the famine came in 1931 the whole world believed that the plan was about to collapse and the Bolshevik regime with it. Contemporaries the world over debated whether the tremendous experiment justified the sacrifice, and whether the famine was not the result of the experiment.

Russian history is filled with famines which were only in part due to crop failures. Those who consider the Socialist state an unnecessary innovation, and believe they could have managed with conservative methods, will condemn Stalin's regime, for it undoubtedly shared in the responsibility for the famine which arose from the resistance of the peasants.

But Stalin had no choice. From the beginning of his dictatorship—that is to say, from the time of the exiling of Trotsky and the removal of all the other leaders of the opposition—a terrific danger lay like an incubus on the new state: the German war. Stalin who, in contrast to Lenin and Trotsky, never believed the world revolution imminent, really understood the utterly antirevolutionary character of the Germans.

A DECADE FOR A CENTURY

It was under such pressure that Russia had to be developed into a rich country by its new colonizers. Never has such a mighty enterprise been carried out under such perilous conditions. Moreover, 150,000,000 helpers had to be fed, encouraged, or pacified while the work was in progress. Fundamentally there was nothing ready, and statistics reveal that in most branches no more was produced in 1928 than in the time of the Czarist regime. To such a degree had the civil war, but also the first Socialist experiment, shattered the country.

If Stalin was to save Socialism and Russia from the threat of war, his first job was to create modern armaments. This depended on coal, iron, and other raw materials, all of which were to be found in Russia. In natural resources the country is actually richer than the United States in water power, and all the other prerequisites for electrification also abounded. To transform these natural treasures into mines and steel mills, to create factories which should serve the purpose of war first and the purposes of peace afterward, would have needed a century in a less scientific age. Not more than a decade was available.

The most important problem was to bring men and mineral deposits together, to merge geology with ethnology. Instead of drawing two separate geologic and political maps, as was formerly done, a new kind of map was thought out. The political order was subordinated to the country's natural wealth not only in general—wheat belt, pasture, coal belt—but also in detail. Science became dictator. The spiritual fanaticism with which science was exalted is unprecedented in world history.

The Czars had not touched the mineral wealth in the country's interior, but had exploited and used the one at the frontiers. In contrast, Stalin, who had experienced the wars of invasion and knew the aggressiveness of the German character, prepared for war. He had also to reckon on air raids, and therefore reversed the Czaristic policy: Constructing the new factories alongside the places where raw materials were found inside of the country, he drew the finished machines and products away from the frontiers, but closer to the consumer. If formerly the two capitals had been surrounded by the chief industrial belts, he now erected chemical works in Taschkent and a plant for silk production in Transcaucasia. He began to drill for oil on the White River—hitherto unexplored—and to distribute it through the whole Ural. The entire Russian output of oil in 1913 had been nine million tons. In 1937 there were 30 million. Today the Russian oil reserves are estimated by geologists at six billion tons.

The American expert, Brooke-Emeny has declared that in case of war—in Russia the main consideration—a blockaded country needed twenty-two kinds of raw materials. Of these Germany and Great Britain lack all but three or four, America lacks nine, but the Soviets only four: tin, nickel, antimony, and tungsten. Therefore they had and still have almost everything; only the Czars exploited it insufficiently, because their sluggish and obtuse state machinery was still driven by steam, while the other countries already made use of electricity. At that time Russia, the sixth part of the world, owned only the fiftieth part of the world's electricity. Twenty years later Stalin erected the Magnet Mountain, one of the largest works on earth, in whose construction thirty-five nations took part.

Stalin availed himself during the first Five Year Plan of Russia's and Asia's streams to exploit with the help of their power the country's wealth and transform it into machines and goods. American engineers finished in 1932 the biggest dam in the world, with which they tamed the Dnieper, as the English had done a generation earlier with the Nile at Assuan. The rapids were conquered, the river made navigable for fifty-five miles, steamships and locks were built, a lake made on the heights. Nearly as much electrical power was generated as in Niagara. Conquered was the Volga with its tributaries through dams and channels. When I sailed downstream there in a miserable boat in 1925, the shore seemed Asiatic, at times biblical. Today a ship can sail from Moscow without reloading into the Black Sea and thence into the Atlantic. Similarly the streams of Siberia were conquered, so that they first generated power and then transported the manufactured goods into other countries on their back. Today New York and Moscow have the largest power stations of all countries on earth.

New York is only mentioned as a symbol. The transformation of Russia into an industrial state can best be compared to the same process in the United States. That it was not only the twentieth century which transformed these countries is proven by the fact that no third example exists—not even Australia.

To this we must add the size and number of inhabitants in both countries—132 to 182 million—which tempts to comparisons. Also in the Soviet Union the most important raw materials were not found at the frontiers. The Ukraine, the Ural, western Siberia, Central Asia, the southern Caucasus—all deep in the country's interior—had never been exploited before the Five Year Plan. At the same time Stalin has united in this decade the most extreme frontier lands of the Union by cutting connections across Asia, just as the United States had done after the Civil War. These railways, converging in central Siberia, have changed the Union into an Asiatic power: a kind of personal victory of Stalin, the Asiatic.

The Russian system, preaching war against the exploiters, has itself been the greatest exploiter of all: but one of nature, not of men. If under the last Czars one-fourth of Russia had been cultivated, this figure has now grown to more than one-half. If there was 43% industry in 1913, we find now after the Five Year Plans 77%. If one considers that the fate of millions of peasants and workingmen is involved in these figures, the tremendous responsibility undertaken by those who decided to change the oldest habits of civilized man and dared to transplant a third of the inhabitants—sixty million—becomes apparent. Under Stalin more than eighty-two major towns with more than 100,000 inhabitants, designed by the most able architects of our time, have sprung up in the Soviet Union: and this in the midst of a traditional peasant's country.

It is true that romantic sentiments will protest against these things and assume that the amount of human happiness destroyed by all this may be greater than the one newly created. But the picture of the pious peasant, living in dull apathy and differentiated from his cattle only by his worship of the icons in the corner, has disappeared, driven away by electric searchlights and roaring passenger airplanes. It will never return again. Perhaps, as some might argue, the increase of the annual industrial output from six to eighty-five billion rubles has nothing to do with God and destiny. Yet there are spiritual achievements which should be added.

Here, where the reconstruction is regulated by the aims of the state, only figures can be given as proof. The Soviets attained under Stalin's rule the first place in the world in regard to tractors, machines, and motor trucks; the second as to electric power. Russia, twenty years ago the least mechanized country, has become the foremost. During the Five Year Plans the entire production of the Soviet Union, increased by 3.8%, constituted 32% of world production. In the same decade between 1929 and 1939, in which the production of all other countries barely mounted, while even dropping in some, Soviet production was multiplied by four. The national income mounted between 1913 and 1938 from twenty-one to one hundred five billion rubles.

The income of the individual citizen was increased by 370% in the last eight years—with only irrelevant income taxes and reasonable social security contributions imposed upon them—while it dropped almost everywhere else in the world. If the standard of life of the Russian farmer is still far below that of the American, we can recognize in what poverty he must have lived under the Czars in a country surpassing all others in natural resources. The peasant, who then owned no leather shoes unless he had inherited them from a lucky father, now received during the second Five Year Plan a pair of them apiece, and before the war even two.

One of the totally paradoxical things in this Socialist state is the production of gold. Here, where gold has at last been abolished as a commodity, where the standard of value is fixed by the people's labor and not by a mass of gold bars dreaming in the dark cellar of some capital of ancient crowns and magicians, more gold is being mined than anywhere else on earth, with the exception of the Transvaal. The same country that combats slavery more persistently than any other one, working for the liberation of the last Portuguese Kaffir sold by his chief to the gold mines of Johannesburg, where he catches tuberculosis and an early death amid the dust of the ore—that country mines, pulverizes, and melts this despised gold. Why? For the sake of dental plates, a few gold cups or jewelry? Only because they have to trade with older states still committed to the gold standard. A Soviet workman helping to produce gold so that foreign goods and weapons may come into the country is a striking symbol for the state of transition in which we are living and which may last for another generation.

The second symbol of Stalin's Five Year Plan—far more cruel and sinister—was motivated by the fact that the entire development had been shaped by the threatening war and consequently begun with war industries. Thus in future times the building of a city may start with erection of air-raid shelters. In order to fabricate tanks and airplanes, this whole people had to restrict itself more and more during these five years; it had to live in greater and greater poverty, lacking everything that makes life pleasant and comfortable. The Russian people resembled a man who, under the stress of danger, cuts down his food so that he may buy a gun.

These privations, far from diminishing the vigor of the Russian youth, tended to increase it. A heightened tempo proved that one can act with "blitzlike" speed without becoming a Fascist. Though wars and famines lowered the enthusiastic mood, it was rekindled to its former revolutionary fervor through the exertions demanded by the Five Year Plan.

Here, too, there were pauses and setbacks; but Stalin's position had gradually become so strong that he could announce the erection of 60% new collective farms, and then reduce the number to 21%. Following Lenin's example, he also made other concessions, tolerating at times even an open market where goods could be privately bought at a twentyfold price and a black stock exchange where the dollar bought forty rubles instead of two.

Though Stalin, in spite of all reverses, refused to take up foreign loans, he was beleaguered by the big banks abroad who recognized that the Russians purchased a tremendous amount of goods and honored their drafts more punctually than democratic Europe. At that time the depression in America stood the Russians in good stead: it nearly replaced a part of the dogmatically announced world revolution. The old states had crisis on crisis, the new socialistic one forged steadily ahead. Stalin, with a plasticity seldom found in his speeches, then said the classic word: "Our difficulties are of such kind that they themselves contain the means of overcoming them." The exciting question continuously lay over him and the Russian people: Who is going to be the swiftest, we or the Germans? Everything depended on the time at which Hitler would seize power or, subsequently, be ready for war! As early as 1935 or not till 1939?

But all this could be carried out only by a youth full of enthusiasm preferring the honors of the pioneer to comfort, and finding ecstasy in a great national aim, not in love of family or romanticism. Perhaps no other generation has ever spent its youth so ceaselessly under the searchlights of a relentless principle. What other nations have been able to endure at the most for a few years under the stress of war —the decline of private life—the Russians have stood for twenty years for the only reason that the glamour of a new idea was made visible and tangible each week through figures, curves and ratios. While the people, during the first five years, were more and more inadequately nourished, housed, and clothed, their enthusiasm was steadily mounting. Stalin has expressed this necessity in one of his speeches:

". . . In order to set technique going," he said, "and to utilize it to the full, we need people who have mastered technique, we need cadres capable of mastering and utilizing this technique according to all the rules of the art. Without people who have mastered technique, technique is dead. Technique in the charge of people who have mastered technique can and should perform miracles. If in our first-class mills and factories, in our Soviet farms and collective farms and in our Red Army we had sufficient cadres capable of harnessing this technique, our country would secure results three times and four times as great as at present. . . .

"It is time to realize that of all the valuable capital the world possesses, the most valuable and most decisive is people, cadres. It must be realized that, under our present conditions, 'cadres decide everything.' If we have good and numerous cadres in industry, agriculture, transport, and the army—our country will be invincible. If we do not have such cadres—we shall be lame on both feet."

It has been suggested that it is the mechanization of mankind as a whole, with its increased productivity, and not the new system, which must take the credit. The fact is, indeed, that ever since Mussolini it has become a device of the dictators to celebrate the opening of every bridge and every railroad station as a stupefying proof of their creative genius. The Russians, too, have known how to exploit every opportunity of this kind. For all that, the difference is fundamental. A ship or a road dedicated by Hitler is proclaimed by his Storm Troops and by his newspapers as a demonstration of the superiority of the master race. There are a million Hitler youths who swallow this in a spirit of complete faith. In Russia the completion of such a work becomes a national event.

The French writer, André Gide has written the most stupid and rancorous words ever said on the Soviets. Not because he turned against them: experienced men of high intellect and subtlety, aided by knowledge and sound arguments, have done the same. But Gide wrote without having the slightest knowledge of the Russian language, landscape, or atmosphere. A decadent, who had never touched real life at any point and does not even understand the technique of travel, he first turned Communist from snobbishness, then, prompted by private disappointments and hurt vanity, anti-Communist after one short trip to Russia. Today the war, however it may end, has gainsaid his shrewdness. In the midst of his other condemnations, Gide also makes fun of the Russian workers, because they always ask: "Have you got anything like this in the West?" When I traveled through Russia, ten years before Gide, I happened to be on the shore of the Black Sea, and suggested to my guide, a Russian student, that we go bathing.

We looked for a spot to leave our clothes. Suddenly the young man saw on the strand a little boat flying the Soviet flag. "Look, there's our boat!" he cried, and sprang into it. In that word "our" was revealed the sense of the state in every citizen, the equivalent of the French king's dictum, "I am the State!" Later on I found in the factories this naïve freshness, this glowing joy in everything that the state —that is, "ourselves"—was accomplishing.

It is numbers that rule, and an entire generation is dissolved in the structure of the state.

But whereas in Germany this idol becomes, under Hitler, a gigantic instrument of domination, in Russia it has become the protection of the masses. In Germany it is feared; in Russia it is now loved as something like a Christmas tree which every one wants to adorn with something.

When the Soviets tried to do away with God, they could find no better substitute than the new state, which became the focus of all the emotions of the youth. The secret of the resistance of the Russian army—that is, of the Russian people—lies in this love for the young state which has been turned over to it, and for the soil which has been turned over to it. Formerly, as the slaves of a ruling caste, the Russians lost three wars in a row. Today they are so young that by comparison with them the United States seems old; they are the youngest nation in the world. This is the achievement of the colonization with which the name of Stalin is associated.

The entire life of the nation was literally absorbed by the two Five Year Plans. No friendship was formed, no marriage consummated, no child born, no work planned without previous consideration whether this would in the tiniest way serve the new reconstruction. The knowledge that now, for the first time, the profit would go not to individuals but to the entire group, the newness of the experiment, fill all the youth and most of the older people with a pride which finds direct expression in production figures. The privations which were imposed on everyone had a stimulating effect, just as they have had in blockaded England. Russia, too, felt itself to be a gigantic fortress which had to arm and defend itself against a threatening enemy, the capitalist system. To be sure, the enemy did not yet rain bombs from the sky, but he bombarded it with an unceasing barrage of derisive or contemptuous articles and books. The effect was to spur the embattled youth on to new achievements.

In this state there developed a sporting impulse which took on a religious aspect. The will of some thousands of workers in one factory to surpass the production of their comrades in another was whipped on by Stalin through the most ingenious devices. The first Five Year Plan was completed in four and a quarter years. If the machines for the first Five Year Plan cost 25 billion rubles, the sum set aside for the same purpose in the second plan amounted to 69.5 billions. Of this total, 53.4 billions were devoted exclusively to heavy industry, while there was a fivefold increase over the first plan in regard to light and food.

The young Russians of both sexes followed these figures with the breathless interest which we associate with a football match, but the remarkable thing was that everyone was a player. It is for this reason that in Russia nothing is more passionately idolized than knowledge and science as the foundation of the new technical state. If in the French Revolution a young actress was paraded and worshiped as the Goddess of Reason, the Russians might have done likewise, but they would have called her the Goddess of Science.

The longing for knowledge, the regard for human life have risen in formerly half-barbarian Russia to the same extent that they have, during the same period, sunk in Germany, the land of spirit and of music. While Hitler methodically dismantled the educational system in order to transfer the youth to the drill ground, while hundreds of German schools had to close, in Russia under Stalin the very towers began to spread knowledge, for they were fitted with loud-speakers. In Germany, before the outbreak of the war, Hitler permitted 60,000 young people to attend the institutions of higher learning; in Russia, Stalin gave permission to 600,000, recruiting young workers and peasants alike as students in newly founded military academies which are today the pride of the country. Hitler drove distinguished scholars out of the country because their fathers had inherited a religion different from the one which he himself does not even believe in. Stalin invited these scholars to his country and gave them important tasks and high salaries. When we consider the care of the aged in Russia, we need only set by its side the answer which a Berlin doctor gave over the telephone to a friend of mine who called for help. He asked how old the patient was, then said: "Seventy! It's no longer worth while! I'm not coming!"

Spiritual attainments, considered of secondary importance by former revolutions and handed out like a tip, have been so generously endowed in the Five Year Plans that their essential value for the whole project becomes apparent. In the budget of western countries the allocations for popular education are swallowed up by the gigantic figures needed for armaments and colonies. In the Soviet Union education and health, houses and books are given first place: under Stalin the expenditure for these things has increased from 30 to 53 billion rubles.

The last statistics published under the Czars has shown that 79% of the population was illiterate. In 1937 this figure had dropped to 10%. Among them were the so-called "wild" people, for instance the Circassians, of whom only 6% could read and write. If the last Czar had sent eight million children to school, Stalin sent twenty-eight. The number of university students increased during twenty years from six hundred thousand to six million. Instead of twenty thousand physicians, there were now one hundred thousand.

If a people's culture has been estimated by the amount of soap it consumes, why not by that of books? While under Hitler the yearly output of German books was cut in half if compared to the preceding decade, the new books appearing each year in Russia have mounted from 87 million in 1913 to 377 million in 1936. Then more books were printed in Russia than in England, Germany, and Japan taken together. Among them were 117 books in 43 foreign languages. The number of newspapers mounted during the Five Year Plans from 859 to 8521, the editions from 3 to 36 million—both a tenfold increase. It may be mentioned that the price of books is so low that each workingman is able to buy three a month for 2% of his wages. The publisher's profit is eliminated, but the author paid extremely well, and so is the artist. The State Prize, awarded to the leading young Soviet composer, Dmitri Shostakovitch for one of his concertos exceeds in its generous height everything the capitalistic world has ever offered to its creative spirits for one single work of genius.

Like the people's education, the exploration of nature is dictated by practical requirements: both are no longer ornament or theory, but necessities for maintaining the state. Books, radio, and film educate the Soviet citizen, who is kept away from banalities and, above all, from obscenities. The scientific institutions enable the rulers to design, and constantly improve, the economic system, distribution of labor, and the entire public life affecting 180 millions. In a country where technology, geology, and chemistry govern the state, Marxism returns to its physical and biologic sources. Within twenty years Stalin has expanded the 211 scientific foundations of 1918 to 2300. These scientists work continuously in the revolutionary spirit in so far as they re-examine everything, reject a great deal, and at the same time exert themselves to the utmost: for science —according to a formula of the foremost chemist—should not follow in the wake of industry, but make discoveries and create new industries. Already Lenin had written the beautiful sentence: "The process of life is creative. It demands a purposefully ordered activity of man."

In Leningrad stands an old palace, in which Czaristic society enjoyed itself not more than thirty years ago. Today the dance hall has become a wheat museum. Here are exhibited 30,000 kinds of wheat, collected and later described by research workers employed by the Soviets. Experimenting for many years, they obtained new crossbreeds between the early maturing wheat of Abyssinia, the hardy one of the northern Caucasus, and that of Afghanistan inured to storms. This enabled them to plant this grain farther north in Russia than heretofore and increase the harvest: at a time when America was burning its wheat. In the same way they succeeded in planting rice, which had never been grown beyond the boundaries of the Po in Europe, in a latitude as far north as London; and to cultivate roses on the shores of Arctic lakes. Crossbreeding, considered so pernicious by the racial philosophy of the Nazis, is one of the most effective Russian means to make men, animals, and plants more productive and beautiful.

Another example given by Johnson, Dean of Canterbury, in his wonderful book on Russia shows how the discovery of an Englishman to make gas from coal seams was never utilized till the Soviets took it up fifty years later. The British coal industry was prompted by business interests to suppress Ramsay's discovery. Not only here, but in all capitalistic countries inventors and explorers have been silenced by buying up at high prices their ideas, which threatened to interfere with monied interests, and then letting them disappear. Lenin recognized that the new method would liberate thousands of miners from injurious toil and bring them from the somber pit into the light laboratory. But many years had to pass till, during the third Five Year Plan, substantial quantities of gas were gained from the coal seams. In those districts, where the method has been applied, one is able today to cook with gas coming immediately out of the ground: a great symbol of our century.

The enthusiasm of the Russian workers found its symbol in Stakhanov. Here was a young miner of the Donets basin who had found a method of turning out, with the help of a pneumatic pick and two timber-men, 102 tons of coal in the six-hour shift of which the regular production had been seven tons. The recognition and application of this discovery followed so swiftly that, overnight, he became a national hero. At the Stakhanov Congress, held only three months later in the Kremlin, he gave this report on himself:

"When I read Comrade Stalin's speech of last May in the Military Academy, and came to the part where he said that in the hands of experts machines could perform miracles, I undertook to increase our production. Now it is a question of installing this system everywhere."

A girl worker in a textile factory reported at the same Congress: "My sister and I went to the manager and said that we wanted to work 100 looms. He gave us ninety-four. Dusya and I were disappointed and insisted on a hundred. When we heard that another weaver was handling 140 looms, we determined to bring the number up to 144. Now we even have plenty of leisure on top of the work. But if someone else goes as high as 144 we're going to raise it to 150, and we shan't let any one else hold the record, if we have to go up to 200."

Immediately before the outbreak of the war the average daily production of the Russian worker was three times what it had been twenty-five years before. Only part of this increase should be credited to the machines; the other part is due to the increased readiness of liberated men to deliver work; and this is the most important factor of all.

When the entire people was called upon to starve so that it might, in the course of a few years, lay the foundations of colonization, there were millions who were dissatisfied, weary, skeptical. The struggle of the rich kulaks who would rather slaughter their cattle than turn them over to the state, the struggle of the middle-class peasants against the poor, held up the advance for years.

And yet the many millions endured for ten years privations which far exceeded those endured by the Germans under Hitler. Since all production is ultimately based on heavy industry, the entire country, which could not or would not import anything, had to do without most consumers' goods. It became a kind of sport to do without things or find substitutes. Like children on Christmas Eve, people wished each other the manufacture of hats or brushes or gloves or bathtubs or radios. The inner history of this period differs from that of Berlin and Rome for the same period in this fundamental respect: there, to the west, two mature and highly cultivated peoples saw themselves almost overnight swindled out of the gifts of life, while here a young people looked forward, across the interval of privation for the sake of a great objective, to the smaller and then the greater pleasures of life.

Here, too, there could be no freedom for the individual. But in Berlin and Rome there was arming for the avowed purpose of conquest, while in Moscow it was for the purpose of defense. In Berlin a people hungered in order to acquire external world domination; in Moscow it hungered in order to build up, internally, a more just society. Hence the moral superiority in the war. If this people is defending itself successfully with the weapons it has only just acquired, the explanation must be sought exclusively in idealistic factors—that is, in the enthusiasm of the laboring and student youth. But as to the outstanding spirits in Russia —they are captivated by the magnificent spectacle in which they are called upon to play their part. Besides, they are very well paid, for in Russia the highest incomes go to the big engineer and the great writer.

The other half of the construction plan was given to the farmer: here still more difficult problems were to be solved. Stalin had to carry out the electrification and mechanization of the farms. It could all be done only by the application of two methods: compulsion where the peasants were concerned, the awakening of enthusiasm where the workers were concerned. The poor or middle-class peasant dreaded collective enterprise. Was Stalin now going to return to the state what he had finally taken from the landlords after three hundred years of slavery? The people were not yet ripe enough to accept the idea of great state farms as the norm, nor was the system sufficiently provided with machines. The peasant distrusted the new form which, he believed, would depress him once more to the level of a day laborer. Even if he had not been, like all peasants everywhere, a conservative, he must still have risen against experiments which he did not understand.

Stalin needed another five years in order to win the confidence of the farmers. This is reflected in the statistics of the increasing millions of collective peasant farms and in the declining numbers of those peasants who died through hunger or rebellion; we see it also in the interminable debates.

The road to this victory was by so much stonier and rougher in the country than in the towns, as a footpath between fields is more uncomfortable than a city boulevard. In the whole world is not the peasant the man most firmly attached to his property? Even if he had been a slave under the Czars—without privileges, without culture, without hope—yet he had owned his shack and his cow, together with a small piece of land. And though he was not allowed to sell it, move away, or marry without his landlord's permission, the few square miles were his home. Here he could torpidly squat amidst squalor and filth.

When the Revolution liberated him after centuries of serfdom, he used this freedom to kill the landlords—unless they had fled—and to take all the land they had owned, or rather dividing it with his neighbors after bloody battles. And now the new masters wanted to take it away again? Wanted to administer the fields collectively? Tilling, sowing, harvesting should be made easier through machinery, but done in common! Thousands were going to be lumped together on big farms belonging to the state!

"But the state, that's you!" explained the Communist speaker. The peasant, feeling that he had been betrayed again, remained sullen. The Communists in the capital understood this only too well. Being sons of peasants themselves, they had experienced the passion with which their fathers had grabbed the land at the beginning of the Revolution. A party report of the year 1923 contains the apt simile: "The peasant is like a sheep. He is shorn by everybody who is in need of wool. First by the Czar and the landlords, then by Denikine and the other armies. Take care, or else we'll have to whistle for wool!"

This sentence voices the tragedy of the Russian peasant during the last thirty years; and also the difficulties under which he was inducted into the Socialist system. This peasant, too, like every other one in the world, was conservative. History has recorded few instances of peasants starting a revolution; mostly they fought against it. In Russia they had been sleeping for several centuries and, soothed by lullabies and prayers for the Little Father (who was anything but a Little Father), had been kept in this state by a reckless hierarchy of avaricious priests and the deified Czar.

The Russian peasant did not even notice any more that he was a slave. One half of all arable land—some people estimated it at 70%—belonged to a few hundred great lords, the Czar, and the Church; the rest was divided among sixteen million peasant families, owning an average of six to eight acres. The methods of cultivating the soil corresponded to this medieval division. For instance, only a sixth of a pound of artificial fertilizer was used per acre, while the Belgian farmer used the hundredfold amount of twenty-one pounds. People were herded together like cattle. The patriarchal benevolence of the big landlords is nothing but a fairytale. Even Count Tolstoi, the humanitarian and poet towering so high above his class, let the peasants on his estate live in squalor. Masaryk, who told me this fact, remonstrated with Tolstoi himself on this account when visiting him in the eighties.

All this is being forgotten or concealed by envenomed men, continuously and fraudulently misrepresenting the Russian liberation as terrorism, because they do not want to give up any of their privileges in their own countries. If this may be understood in the case of rich persons who have either toiled for their wealth or inherited it without effort, it becomes unpardonable in the case of spiritually endowed men who should be enabled through their talent and culture to comprehend the grandeur of this movement. The house of any poet taking a stand against it is nothing but an ivory tower which cannot withstand the whirlwind of this age. Many things were beautiful in the old world, and it is not by chance that each epoch looks on the preceding one as the good old times. But anyone in a position to compare a Russian farmstead of 1910 with one of 1930 must confess that the latter guarantees more of two all-important elements: human happiness and dignity.

Not through the Communists, but through the violent inroads of western powers, who had no business in Russia, the country had become involved in ever greater wars and disasters. The main issue was not so much the introduction of the Socialist system as the salvation of the country through the new leaders. It was not a handful of doctrinaires and dreamers who ruined the country, but the heads of international banks and industrial establishments who, by means of the governments they controlled, sent their armies to the country of dangerous experiments in order to save their oil and their investments, and at the same time suppress any imitations at home. They tried to do exactly the same thing in France in 1790, and still lost the war in the end.

Had the accession of the Communists in Russia been nothing but the victory of a faction, it would have been no event of world-wide significance. Only the fact that the Communists raised Russia out of its cultural depth and at the same time set an example to the world, made their work so important. "Russia," wrote Stalin, "has always been beaten because of its backwardness. It was beaten by the Mongolian Khans. It was beaten by the Turkish Beys and the Swedish noblemen. . . . We have inherited a backward country, which we found in a complete state of collapse after four years of war and three years of civil war—a country with a primitive system of production where industry was only an oasis in the desert of an economic life dominated by the petty bourgeois."

But the civil war did not mark the end of the fighting. Famines were renewed through the resistance of the rich peasants, so that this country, with its immense wheat production, had to import grain from Argentine. Similarly, this same country, with its immense army, had entered the World War without fervor and had therefore been quickly defeated, though it was allied with the victors. Stalin's battle against the rich peasants, who did not want to give up their wheat, was necessary in spite of the terrific number of victims. Thousands of rich peasants who defended their cattle, sometimes also their gold, in groups or singly on each farmstead, were murdered. Most of this happened in 1928, just before the first Five Year Plan. Caught between the famine in the towns and the danger of being ousted by the reactionaries, Stalin had to resort to terrorism. Only force could overcome this chaotic condition in many parts of the Russian peasant districts. After this, it was again need which gave birth to the great plan.

In addition, the battle between the single classes of the peasants themselves made the plan and reconstruction still more difficult. Who was a peasant of "medium means" and who a poor one? If a man had two horses, two cows, and an old shack, he was perhaps poorer than one owning one horse, one cow, and a new cottage. Sometimes he might join the ranks of the rich, sometimes that of the poor.

Another hindrance lay in the bureaucracy which was ingrained in the Russian character and could not be immediately dissolved after three hundred years. Like the secret police, it has been inherited from the Czars, and is still in existence. And now, in the face of all these obstructions, a new system had to be suddenly enforced, liquidating the new wealth in the country—as had been done with the old one before—and working for the good of the poor.

A hecatomb of victims! Innumerable acts of injustice in order to found a new justice! Force everywhere in order to abolish force! The same old tragedy, which had begun with the decision of Amenophis, the first revolutionary, three thousand and a half years ago! Already the number of victims during the civil war had been estimated at four millions. But those falling six years later excited more horror, because at that time the new state had already been consolidated, and now seemed shaken again. When the rich peasants were forced to join the state or collective farms, they revenged themselves in typical peasant manner. As they had no guns, they slaughtered their cows and pigs, preferring to eat them up to letting the state seize them. Sometimes they stuffed themselves so full that they died of the consequences. Many such symbolic tragicomedies were told later on.

Salvation came through the tractor. When it began, with its mighty wheels, blades, and prongs, to plow up the ancient soil; to cut, stack, and transport the harvest, it seemed like a fantastic monster to the peasants. But soon the tractor became the new saint, and thus it has remained till today. The old people, who did not want to believe in it, died out. In a Moscow museum intended to ridicule the clergy with its supplications for rain, I talked to an old woman who was supposed to guide the visitors and point out the pictures explaining the processes of nature. On one side was the Lord, descending in the tempest to inflict punishment on man, on the other side the concussion of two electric currents. The old woman smiled and said: "My son believes in the new things, but I don't." Old miracle stones and talismans, which were kept under glass as relics of a religiousness belonging to the past, received the visits of unknown people who still worshiped them secretly in the old way.

The tractor had become the new saint. "In order to preserve Russia," Lenin had written, "we need more than good harvests and minor industries. Without major industries we can never become independent." Stalin, who founded the Five Year Plan on this thought, announced the following principle: "Frankly and stubbornly, we must put farming on a technical basis and achieve large-scale production, keeping step with socialistic industry. If we solve this question, victory will be ours. If not, we shall be pushed back into capitalism."

The truth was that victory depended on self-sufficiency; for from the west threatened the German, waxing ever stronger, from the east the Japanese. These invasions were bound to come and destroy the new state, unless it was prepared. The dilemma grew, because major industry and agrarian management not only depended on each other,

but were also competitors. It was impossible to do everything at the same moment. And still it was imperative that
everything should be done at once.

Inasmuch as Russia was an agrarian country, Socialism
could triumph only if it increased the harvests by the use
of machinery and mass production. "Our difficulty," wrote
Lenin in the first stages, "lies in the fact that we are beginning our revolution in a country of peasants who everywhere in the world insist passionately on private ownership." Stalin, half peasant by origin, added: "The peasant
is not going to be driven to Socialism by any mystical
phrase, but only by his self-interest. If we show him that
with commonly owned machines he can harvest more and
earn more, he will accept it."

Finally the peasants, partly forced and partly convinced,
really accepted what had been offered to them. They began to understand the phrase *"L'état, c'est moi,"* in its relation to themselves. Thus there developed inside of twenty
years a self-confidence the like of which is to be found in
no democratic European peasant, but only in the American, who has never been oppressed. It is true that things
on the farms moved more slowly than in industry. While
the workingman was used to joint labor, the stubbornness
of the peasant who lived alone or with his sons stood in
the way of progress. Had the former been impressed by
the fact that everyone could find work, this inspiring
reason did not affect the latter who had never been out
of work.

Thus Stalin initiated the work on the farms by providing the weightiest and most expensive implements. As the Lord had first created the elements, then tamed them, then populated and cultivated the earth, and finally brought forth man, so these small divinities had first to tame the rivers so that they would furnish electric power, then dig with the help of this power into the soil's interior so that coal and ore might come forth, then construct big plants where machines could be produced, and finally build tractors with these machines. Not till then could the peasant's son climb on the driver's seat and guide the tractor across the field on which his forefathers had worked with their own hands and which was now furrowed, planted, and leveled by the iron monster. Was it a miracle that the millions had to lack clothes, shoes, houses in the first stage? It was more of a miracle that they did not revolt.

After the first ten years of the plans were over, the picture had brightened on the farms. Now Stalin was already able to make the following demands: "Each district must have its own agricultural output in order to produce its own vegetables, butter, milk, and, if possible, also its own wheat and meat." Thus, under his regulating hands, corn wandered to the east, wheat to the north, and cotton to the south. In the north of the gigantic country, forests, swamps, and moors were transformed into arable land, in the south deserts.

In Central Asia, where the Czars had tried to grow cotton, but had been deadlocked by their bureaucratic methods, enough cotton is being produced today to provide twice the number of inhabitants with clothes. A modern system of traffic and transportation has been created connecting the industrial centers of the U.S.S.R. with her agricultural regions by railroads, highways, canals, and air lines. Camels and horses, who still today turn grating wheels on the Nile to water the plantations, have been replaced by pumps. The best seeds and kinds have been planted, so that the crop can compete with the one grown in Egypt.

Stalin's enduring merit in history, despite all the bloody sacrifices, consists of a practical creation of the first Socialist state by industry, the effects of which express themselves in the raising of the standard of life of workers and peasants throughout the whole world under the threatening pressure and example of the Soviets.

Three reproaches have been leveled at Stalin and his Soviets: that they are antipatriotic, that they take away everyone's property, and that they repress every individual's intelligence in a universal equalization. All three are false.

Love of the fatherland has, under Stalin's regime, been cultivated to a point of nationalism, which proves itself indomitable under Hitler's most brutal attack. Expropriation was applied against owners of estates who, in the beginning of the Revolution, neither had acquired nor maintained their land by their own labor and who, in the spirit of our time, must give way to such as come by the work of hand or brain under Goethe's famous dictum:

STALIN AGAINST EQUALIZATION

"Wouldst thou possess thy heritage, essay
By earning it, to render it thine own."

Later, in 1919 and 1928, the battle against the rich farmer was taken up again. What had been accomplished here by blood and force, was realized in England and America without blood and force, by taxing property up to 80%.

As regards the fable of equalization, we find that it had been derided by Marx, Lenin, and Stalin alike. In the land which has raised science to the status of a divinity, superior talent, higher education, and greater application are better rewarded in money and honor than anywhere else in the world. As the western world has taken pleasure in reproaching the Soviets successively that they applied too much or too little equalization, I asked Stalin how the newly introduced piecework, implying an uneven wage scale, could be reconciled with Marxian principles. He answered:

"A completely socialized state, where all receive the same amount of bread and meat, the same kind of clothes, the same products, and exactly the same amounts of these products—such a Socialism was not recognized by Marx. Marx merely says that so long as the classes are not entirely wiped out, and so long as work has not become a pleasure —for now most people look upon it as a burden—there will be many people who would like to have others do more work than they. So long, then, as the distinction of class is not entirely obliterated, people will be paid according to their productive efficiency, each according to his capacity. That is the Marxist formula for the first stage of Socialism. When Socialism has reached the completed stage, everyone will do what he is capable of doing, and for the work he has done will be paid according to his needs.

"It should be perfectly clear that different people have different needs, great and small. Marx himself attacks the principle of equalization. That is a part of primitive peasant psychology, not Socialism."

There is something downright comical in the way Stalin's opponents, confronted by the staggering triumph of Russian reconstruction, have reproached him for having betrayed Socialism and revealed himself as nothing more than a dreary entrepreneur in the old style. In reality, Stalin, like Lenin before him, has honestly maintained the fundamental principle of Socialism, namely, the nationalization of production and of foreign trade. As regards the soil, however, there has not been much more nationalization in Russia than in Italy, where one third of the land already belongs to the Fascist state. But Stalin, again like Lenin before him, adapted the methods and forms of Socialism to changing circumstances from year to year. It was only thus that he could have carried out the two great plans.

A colonizer cannot be held in leash by a dogma, but a genuine revolutionary will never betray his fundamental principles. Avoiding both dangers, Stalin has courageously gone his way and reached a goal, which up to now had been considered Utopian by history.

THE MAGIC MAP

At the Congress of 1929 a speaker submitted from the platform the first Five-Year Plan, and as he indicated on a large map of the Union the places where new power centers were to be erected, small electric lights sprang out one after another. As he touched on the planned foundries, mines, oil wells, textile factories, lights of different colors illustrated each enterprise. When the speaker finally pointed to the glowing map and said softly and as if incidentally, "This is what we are fighting for," a storm of enthusiasm swept through the audience. Tears came into the speaker's eyes.

What must have been Stalin's emotions when he had the map lit up once more four years later! In every spot where a lamp glowed, there was now real light.

CHAPTER SIX

The Legislator

Through buildings and through laws leaders of nations insure themselves that their memory will be honored by posterity. Their own generation, their subjects or cocitizens do not thank them for these achievements. They consider no freedom great enough, no security sure enough, no cathedral beautiful enough. They criticize everything and are always dissatisfied. Contemporaries are impressed by conquest, luck, prosperity. Posterity understands that all this is transitory and clings to the only things bequeathed by the conquerors after their empires have been annihilated and their peace treaties annulled: domes and towers, façades and bridges, dams and channels carry the names of Roman emperors and French kings to future times. Nobody, on hearing the name of Justinian, who was one of the greatest rulers, remembers anything but his laws. Washington, a national figure, excites far less interest outside of America than Jefferson, who formulated a new principle for humanity.

Nothing has outlived Napoleon except a portrait, a legend, and the *Code Napoléon*. Portrait and legend belong together, showing him almost always as general, more seldom as ruler, never as legislator. And yet his constructive genius, which separates him so completely from his small present-day imitators, emerges nowhere as clearly as in the laws with which he abolished an anarchy of ten years—and this with the pen amid a conclave of wise men. It will never be forgotten that this soldier and adventurer, during the same night in which he seized power through bayonets and cannons, appointed two commissions to work out that code of laws which the Revolution had failed to give to the people for ten years. Through this symbolic act the general tried to atone for his violent deed and the perpetrated injustice by restituting public law.

Justinian and Napoleon, the two great legislators of the Christian era, were autocrats and generals, sacrificed thousands to their ideas of personal power, and yet hastened to give those laws that were destined to survive their conquests. Here a secret restlessness seemed to drive them to action. The two emperors, both upstarts of bourgeois descent, ordered the working out of legal codes immediately after they had grasped the power. Both have contributed decisions which, reaching deep into the life of their own and subject nations, have persisted till today. A woman seeking divorce in the year 1942 in Argentine or Egypt is guided by the ideas of marriage or paternal rights formulated by Napoleon one century and Justinian fourteen centuries ago.

Both legislators needed only fourteen and eighteen

months, respectively, for their work; while other codes took thirty years and the international laws in the Hague could not be formulated within a period of twenty years. It is not certain whether the Roman emperor took as active a part in the legislation as the French: Napoleon presided at ninety-seven meetings out of one hundred two held by the commission. These meetings often did not begin till nine in the evening and were preceded by a day devoted by the First Consul to a gigantic amount of work. Once, when one of the consultants went to sleep, the Consul shook him and said: "Wake up, citizen! We must earn our salary!"

It is just as easy to find the contradictions between the public acts of a legislating king and his legal directions as to contrast a philosopher's system with his love life. By their doctrines and prescriptions both try to overcome those weaknesses and tendencies in themselves into which human nature ever falls back. Justinian, who abolished the Roman Consulate—the foundation of a thousand-year-old constitution—by force, formulated at the same time great principles of justice and distributed them through the whole world. Napoleon, who sacrificed the rights of man hundreds of times to his conquests, yet codified the foundations of these rights and realized for the first time the ideas of the great revolution within an ancient kingdom: abolishment of hereditary nobility; equal rights for all classes and races, including the Jews; civil marriage and divorce for everybody alike.

After he had instituted his code in almost all of Europe, from Warsaw to Paris, from Copenhagen to Naples—and even as far as Louisiana—the subject nations tried to repeal it after his defeat. In vain! People everywhere returned to its principles; and today, one hundred forty years after its completion, the *Code Napoléon* regulates the legal life of half of Europe and of twenty-five nations outside, especially in South America. This could only happen because it was conceived in neither a nationalistic nor polemic spirit, but embodied the new principles of the era: the thoughts of the encyclopedists.

Greater than lawbooks are constitutions in the history of mankind; greater than constitutions the manifestos fixing the moral foundations of public justice.

In the middle of the period between Justinian and Napoleon, the English produced the greatest paper of this sort: the Magna Carta Libertatis of 1215. It guaranteed for the first time plain, full rights for the underdog, so that he would not any more become prisoner or exile without his legitimate judge and law. This first great paper of liberty was acknowledged thirty-two times by the English, in a period of three hundred years; later on, during four hundred years, by the whole western mankind. It was only Adolf Hitler who found a nation which accepted the abolition of these old rights of men.

The Magna Carta has a much greater place in the history of mankind than the Bill of Rights of 1689. This Bill speaks of nothing but the rights of Parliament against the kings, confers freedom of speech only on Parliament, creates no new law and is important only in one of its thirteen paragraphs, the freedom of election.

A century later Jefferson, perhaps the greatest American, wrote with his small, deft handwriting the page initiating the history of the modern state. In this he has only codified what thinkers before him, what Rousseau and Locke, had formulated and postulated. Furthermore this famous document is filled to a great part with accusations against a king who has been completely forgotten, with reasons for a defection no longer of interest to anybody. Its permanent value does not lie in the fact that it declares the independence of a new state, but in its form and reasoning. It was an event in history that a state established itself on the basis of democratic idealism and expressed the fundamental principle: "That all men are created equal, that they are endowed, by their Creator, with certain unalienable rights, that among these are life, liberty, and the pursuit of happiness." For the first time a nation had expressed that each act of the government was dependent on the consent of the governed.

In this sense Jefferson's document is much more significant than the constitution which followed eleven years later and whose ponderous style does not differentiate it much from other constitutions. After the Declaration of Independence it brought to the world only the realization of the same principles, with the exception of the famous First Amendment: "Congress shall make no law respecting an establishment of religion or prohibiting the free exercise thereof." The word God, which Jefferson replaced by the word Creator, is not mentioned in this Constitution. Even the oath of the President begins only with the words: "I do solemnly swear . . . ."

France and the United States sent their slogans to each other across the ocean, simplified or multiplied them on the other coast, sounded them anew, and thus returned them to the mother country in rejuvenated form. For the people's sovereignty, demanded by Voltaire and Rousseau, had been realized in America for the first time. But immediately afterward a messenger from France brought proofs of the idealism flowering there anew: Lafayette composed the "Droits de l'Homme," whose seventeen articles combine the logic of the French language with the pathos of its spirit and represent the finest document ever produced by the political mind of man since the Greeks and the Renaissance. This document, following the American constitution after two years and preceding the French by two, leads, in the riches of its text, all programs of modern liberty.

The Paris constitution of 1791, emphasizing the rights of man, makes in many details concessions to the old bourgeois world. Here equality was stabilized only before the law, not in regard to education; and the moneyed classes were granted many advantages. The socialistic laws were mainly intended as war measures and soon disappeared in practice. Property was explicitly guaranteed. At the same time the universal principle was changed imperceptibly, as it was under the fingers of the legislators, into a national one. All the speakers of the convention spoke of the liberty they were going to bring to the oppressed nations—if necessary, by force; and Danton called the Rhine the natural boundary of France which would have to be captured. Despite this, the fundamental feeling, in its relationship to the rights of man, remained a humane one.

The third great document of modern humanity, after the Declaration of Independence and the Paris Rights of Man, is represented by the Soviet Constitution of 1936. In the interim, during the last one hundred sixty years, nothing is to be found in which the nineteenth century had reached, or even anticipated, the moral height of the eighteenth or twentieth; for the Communist Manifesto is only a program for a new system of economics.

History will call this new constitution by the name of Stalin, though he did not head the Soviet Union, but only the Communist party at the time of its inception, and though its main thoughts had been already formulated by Lenin in his first two constitutions of 1918 and 1924. All great constitutions are short, those of America and the Soviets each comprising twenty-four pages. It is equally hard to wade through either of them. Such documents resemble gold ore whose grayness disappoints the miner till a lucky glance reveals the slender gold deposit. And yet the entire gigantic rock is famous and precious only for the sake of these narrow veins.

In the Soviet constitution these deposits are more plentiful than anywhere else since the Paris Rights of Man. It is only amazing that it took so much longer in the present

than in the past to realize this new state philosophy. Voltaire lived to see the great revolution, but very few Russian
revolutionaries can recall the times of Marx. Between his
book and this constitution lies half a century. Marx had
formulated this principle for the new state: "From each
according to his ability, to each according to his work."
Engels had added: "Government over persons will be replaced by the administration of objects and production.
The state will not be abolished, but it will wither away."
Lenin had expressed the same idea differently: "Every cook
will have to learn how to govern."

These fundamental thoughts were already realized in
Lenin's first constitutions, but not promulgated on a large
scale before Stalin. A legislation is never a novel creation.
Always, since the days of the Babylonian code, it has been
a formulation of already existing or newly stabilized state
morality. The idea of the Soviets is founded on the right
to work and the duty to work. It is a great symbol that the
Communist state of the twentieth century has taken over
one of the principles of the oldest communist communities, that of the apostolic Christians of the first century,
word for word. St. Paul says (II Thessalonians, 3,10):
"Even when we were with you, this we commanded you:
If any man will not work, neither let him eat." Soviet
Constitution, Article II: "In the Union work is the duty of
each able citizen after the principle: He does not work,
neither shall he eat."

This categorical obligation, up to now imposed by no
state on its citizens, is balanced through the equally new

duty of the state: "The citizens of the union have the right to work, the right to be guaranteed a job and pay for their work, according to its value and amount. The right to work is assured through the socialistic system of economics."

Still greater appears at first sight the difference from the American constitution in regard to property: the latter guaranteeing it, the former abolishing it. In spite of this, the development of both state forms will lead them toward each other. Not the constitution, but practical requirements have brought America, in accordance with the new age, closer to the Russian dogma. While here public utilities have been taken over more or less by the state, property in Russia has been abolished only in limited fashion. Here the constitution says: "The Soviet Union is founded on the principle that ownership of the means of production and exploitation of one man by the other must be abolished."

In the United States a number of rivers, farms, mines, forests, dams, and power stations are owned by the state today: that is they are the property of the whole nation. In the constitution of the Soviets the corresponding article, of course greatly enlarged, says the following: The land and all it contains—rivers, forests, mills, factories, mines, railways, means of transportation by water and air, dams, roads, state farms, storage places for machinery and tractors, as well as the main dwellings found in towns and industrial centers—are owned by the state, that is they are the property of the whole nation. On the other hand, private property is partly retained by the Soviets, for it says further on: "The personal property of the citizens derived from their work, savings made in their households, and objects for personal use and comfort are protected by law." This protection is executed on the farms in a personal way, and the Soviet constitution is probably the first in the world to mention poultry, in the following way: "Each householder on a collective farm shall own a piece of land as individual property for his personal use, in addition the house, livestock, poultry and smaller implements. . . . Outside of the socialistic system, the law permits smaller private farms and other undertakings founded on personal work and excluding the exploitation of others."

For the principles of public ownership and the duty to work have their deep moral foundation in the new and revolutionary thoughts of the Soviets tending to hinder the exploitation of man by man. Where private ownership has been abolished, the privilege of the private owner to become a millionaire through low wages and high prices has been abolished, too. In this way the striving for gold as the greatest aim in life becomes impossible, while the striving for the good things of life, in recompense of diligence and talent, is retained. Where exploitation of human labor has been prohibited, but private property and savings permitted to a limited degree, life will offer a new purpose.

Thus the protection of the state is granted not only the "proletarian," but every citizen, because no extremely rich or poor man can exist. Together with the right to work each citizen is guaranteed the following things: gratuitous education, access to all cultural advantages, paid vacations, insurance against sickness and old age.

The difference in the standard of life is only determined by the ability of the single man. The external glamour of life, enjoyed in all other countries by a few big business-men or rich heirs, has been sacrificed to a feeling of security guaranteed by no other state to its citizens. In order to remove the fear of the vacuum endured by 90% of the citizens, the enjoyment of the other 10% must be curtailed. Then the worker will not be filled any more by hate and jealousy, nor the owner by hate and fear of revolts. From then on a new division of sentiments within the community may begin to develop.

Labor has replaced money as standard of value. The gold standard of the old states has been substituted by the efficiency standard of the new state. The way to the goods of this world is opened neither by the number of gold bars kept by each man in his cellar or, in the form of currency, in the bank, nor by the accidents of birth and inheritance; but merely by the individual's own accomplishments leading to a greater or lesser gratification of material or ideal desires. The beginning of each human life is as equal economically as physically. Its end is completely unequal, in accordance with each man's attainments.

Such a state without classes must necessarily be a state without races. Privileges for any race or color are explicitly denied by the constitution: "Every direct or indirect diminution of the rights of races or nations, every direct or indirect privilege claimed by races or nations, as well as the defense of special racial or national rights and hate or discrimination against any race are punishable by law." In the same weeks of the year 1936 in which this constitution was made known to the Russian people, Hitler announced his Nuremberg laws against the Jews.

The warlike character of the Russian statute became apparent to the world. The plan of the new constitution had been discussed and criticized in the whole country for six months. At the same time universal, direct, and equal suffrage was instituted and the people instructed through speeches and articles.

Two parties were formed for this first vote which was going to decide on the constitution: the Communists, and the Non-Party block. When Stalin described to the people on the day before the balloting the type of politician whom they should vote for, he was clever enough to paint an idealized portrait of Lenin and not of himself. Ninety millions voted for, but four millions against the constitution.

Here, as everywhere else, there were contradictions between theory and practice. Though the same freedom of speech and written word is guaranteed in Russia as in America, this privilege cannot be always used there in as free a manner as here. But where in the world has a constitution ever been carried out to the end? Have the rights of men been realized? Do the Negroes in the United States enjoy the same rights as the white man? No legislation is able to transform a revolutionary principle into reality a hundred per cent.

We must be satisfied with the fact that as world historic an event as the acceptance of this constitution amid a virtual party dictatorship could be declined by four million voters. Generally kings and dictators have surrendered only a fraction of one per cent in their plebiscites in order to gain added luster by stressing the voters' apparent independence.

The great state documents of the modern age—the Declaration and Constitution of Philadelphia, the Rights of Man, and the *Code Napoléon* of Paris—have now been joined by Stalin's Constitution of Moscow which is going to make his name more immortal than anything else he has done, even if he should be able to sign the peace treaty in Berlin as victor.

CHAPTER SEVEN

On Terror

One evening—it was in 1930—I heard Tschaikowsky's *Pique Dame* in the Moscow Opera. Stalin sat in a box, and it was said that he was attending the wonderful performance for the fourth time. In the fourth act we were shown the square before the Winter Palace, the residence of the Czars in old Petersburg, illuminated by night, while snow fell and six soldiers marched on guard before the gate till the relief came, commands rang through the night, and new soldiers mounted guard. For a hundred years this had gone on before that gate.

As I was going home in my sleigh an hour later, we cut across the Red Square which, under tremendous floodlights, was bounded by the Kremlin walls, while within the towers rose into the dim winter sky. It was December, and snow was falling heavily. Before Lenin's mausoleum by the Kremlin wall the sentinels paced. Six men striding back and forth till the relief came, commands rang through the night, and new soldiers mounted guard. Since all we saw were overcoats, boots, and hats, the men looked exactly like the ones in the opera. A hundred years after the period depicted in the opera the same shadows came striding out of the snow, before the same gate of power. Within that gate, in his glass coffin, lay the predecessor of that new Czar whom I had seen only a few moments ago filled with such delight by the picture of the ancient form of power which he had helped to destroy.

Overwhelmed by the repetition I got back into the sleigh and asked myself whether the whole bloody sacrifice which the revolution had exacted had been worth while, and I could not answer that question.

Placed practically on top of these events, we must project them to a distance. When we study ancient history, the best thing to do is to use opera glasses to bring it nearer; when we study modern history we must turn the glasses round, so that the nearer appears far off. The French and the American Revolutions, of which the Russian one was the great continuation, cost many more human lives than were counted.

What remains? Before the naïve force of legend the sacrifices disappear in the course of one century, but the achievements reveal increasing greatness. The highest European spirits, who greeted the Great Revolution of 1789 with blazing enthusiasm, averted their eyes from it in horror when the Terror began. And yet it is on the French Revolution that the structure of our modern states is erected. All the civic liberties which Europe enjoyed in the century between Napoleon's finish and Mussolini's beginning, stem from the French Revolution. It is symbolic that Fascism should specifically negate them.

Whoever considers human happiness, and not power, as the aim of every political order will feel that his enthusiasm for the Russian Revolution is dimmed again and again by somber emotions. I wanted to hear the so-called "Bloody Czar" himself talk about the terror, and include a part of our conversation, such as it was then published in Russia with Stalin's permission.

"You have led the life of a conspirator for such a long time," I said to Stalin; "and do you now think that, under your present rule, illegal agitation is no longer possible?"

"It is possible, at least to some extent."

"Is the fear of this possibility the reason why you are still governing with so much severity, so many years after the Revolution?"

"No. I will illustrate the chief reason for this by giving a few historical examples. When the Bolsheviks came to power they were soft and easy with their enemies. At that time, for example, the Mensheviks (Moderate Socialists) had their lawful newspapers and also the Social Revolutionaries. Even the military cadets had their newspapers. When the white-haired General Krasnov marched upon Leningrad and was arrested by us, under the military law he should have been shot or at least imprisoned, but we set him free on his word of honor. Afterward it became clear that with this policy we were undermining the very system we were endeavoring to construct. We had begun by making a mistake. Leniency toward such a power was a crime against the working classes. Then we realized that the only way to get ahead was by the policy of absolute severity and intransigence. The illegal campaigns which we ourselves had carried on in the old days were naturally valuable to us as an experience, but that was not the decisive factor."

"This policy of cruelty," I answered, "seems to have aroused a very widespread fear. In this country I have the impression that everybody is afraid and that your great experiment could succeed only among this long-suffering nation that has been trained to obedience."

"You are mistaken," said Stalin, "but your mistake is general. Do you think it possible to hold power for so long merely by intimidating the people? Impossible. The Czars knew best how to rule by intimidation. It is an old experiment in Europe and the French bourgeoisie supported the Czars in their policy of intimidation against the people. What came of it? Nothing."

"But it maintained the Romanovs in power for three hundred years."

"Yes, but how many times was that power shaken by insurrections? To forget the older days, recall only the revolt of nineteen-five. Fear is in the first instance a question of the mechanism of administration. You can arouse fear for one or two years and through it, or at least partly through it, you can rule for that time. But you cannot rule the peasants by fear. Secondly, the peasants and the working classes in the Soviet Union are by no means so timid and long-suffering as you think. You believe that our people are timid and lazy. That is an antiquated idea. It was believed in formerly, because the landed gentry used to go to Paris to spend their money there and do nothing. From this arose an impression of the so-called Russian laziness. People thought that the peasants were easily frightened and made obedient. That was a mistake. And it was a threefold mistake in regard to the workers. Never again will the workers endure the rule of one man. Men who have reached the highest pinnacles of fame were lost the moment they had got out of touch with the masses. Plechanov had great authority in his hands, but when he became mixed up in politics he quickly forgot the masses. Trotsky was a man of great authority, but not of such high standing as Plechanov, and now he is forgotten. If he is casually remembered, it is with a feeling of irritation."

I did not intend to mention Trotsky to Stalin but since he himself had broached the subject, I asked: "Is the feeling against Trotsky general?"

"If you take the active workers, nine tenths speak bitterly of Trotsky." (We spoke before the Moscow trials, in December 1931.)

There was a short pause during which Stalin laughed quietly and then took up the thread of the question again: "You cannot maintain that people may be ruled for a long time merely by intimidation. I understand your skepticism. There is a small section of the people which is really afraid. It is an unimportant part of the peasant body. That is represented by the kulaks. They do not fear anything like the initiation of a reign of terror but they fear the other section of the peasant population. This is a hang-over from the earlier class-system. Among the middle classes, for example, and especially the professional classes, there is something of the same kind of fear, because these latter had special privileges under the old regime. Moreover, there are traders and a certain section of the peasants that still maintain the old liking for the gentry.

"But if you take the progressive peasants and workers, not more than fifteen per cent are skeptical of the Soviet power, or are silent from fear or are waiting for the moment when they can undermine the Bolshevik state. On the other hand, about eighty-five per cent of the more or less active people would urge us further than we want to go. We often have to put on the brakes. They would like to stamp out the last remnants of the intelligentsia. But we would not permit that. In the whole history of the world there never was a power that was supported by nine tenths of the population as the Soviet power is supported.

"That is the reason for our success in putting our ideas into practice. If we ruled only by fear, not a man would have stood by us. And the working classes would have destroyed any power that attempted to continue to rule by fear. Workers who have made three revolutions have had some practice in overthrowing governments. They would not endure such a mockery of government as one merely based on fear."

Since this conversation the Five Year Plans have produced such great results in Russia that criticism has become fainter. We are all inclined to forget the victims in the face of victory, though this should be permitted to neither moralist nor philosopher. Even the Moscow trials appear in a different light since Stalin has been fending off the same German armies which some of the Bolshevists sentenced at that time wanted to call into the country.

In addition, dictatorship must take on a different aspect in wartime, because it is bound to increase everywhere, be it in veiled or open form. The Romans, who invented a name and provisions for the emergencies of war and disaster, gave such unlimited powers to their functionaries, but only for six months. Stalin has summoned the Soviet Congress, which had convened each year up to 1925, only twice in the next five years. Consequently the highest organ of the state assembles but rarely; and twenty whips see to it that Congress reappoints the General Secretary of the Communist Party again and again.

These questions of dictatorship and terrorism remain awake in every heart. Therefore the feelings of men who formerly fought with him or deserted him are important for our judgment. Only they must not be frustrated Stalins resembling those frustrated Hitlers who strut around in foreign countries because their model defeated or banished them.

Here I include the most significant statement—given by a writer who tried to be just, here quoted from Levine—which I could discover within the circle of the disappointed: Dimitrievsky.

S. Dimitrievsky with his clarity—without love but evidently also without hate—who had been a high Soviet official, member of the embassy in Stockholm for many years and later a voluntary exile, is important as witness and antagonist. But this book shows why, in some points, we cannot agree with the following description of Stalin.

"Stalin is a very decent man. He lives like an ascetic. He works like a giant. To govern Russia sitting on bayonets, and on the shoulders of an unreliable bureaucracy, is not easy. Iron will is needed to bear the ceaseless inner struggle with those near him, as well as with the population of a vast country, and to mark that course which extends a new lease of life to Stalin and his order, and which bars the way to the next pretender. There are many hands reaching for the scepter of Russian autocrat—for Stalin, if not literally, nevertheless holds this scepter. And these hands are all sinuous, their muscles are strong, there is ample blood on them, and it is not a light affair to keep them off. . . .

"Enormous will power, great experience, clear thinking are needed for the job—regardless of the historical correctness or incorrectness of the course taken. Unquestionably Stalin is greater than all his competitors in the struggle for power.

"That he has remained so long in the shadows made a deep impression in the country with Eastern conceptions, where despots have always kept themselves behind thick walls. This created for him a mysteriousness. It gave rise to a belief among sincere people that Stalin seeks nothing for himself. But he has nothing to seek, for he has everything. He understood the secret of power: not the eulogies of admirers, not the enthusiasm of the mob. He knows that tomorrow that mob may cry: 'Crucify him!' that tomorrow his friends may desert him.

"Power rests on bayonets, in an obedient machine, in managing people, in playing on their desires, in a political police, in a system of country-wide espionage and strangulation. That it is possible to govern by moral and intellectual persuasion Stalin does not believe.

"Stalin knows that the majority of his collaborators hate him. But he suffers them, works with them, relies on them, for he holds them in his grip, and he knows that in spite of their hatred they will bend before him and carry out his will. That they will denounce him behind his back is of no account to him.

"In every public address, Stalin shows clearly what he wants. He does not like to make people think, and he saves them the trouble. I believe that in time it will be recognized that Stalin as a writer and thinker was an uncommon man.

"It is said that Stalin has no original thoughts, that he steals others' ideas. Even if it were so, it takes ability to sift all kinds of opinions and organize the selections in the course of a great political game—all the time hanging over an abyss, maneuvering between shoals and reefs. Stalin is not a theoretician. He is a promoter endowed with great intuition.

"He is an Oriental statesman of the type of government where one or a few primitive minds think for the even more primitive mass. Without nerves, without sweep, he is a terrible dominating force, appearing often not as a human being but as a machine.

"Stalin is a great nationalist, not of the future Russia, but of Communist Eurasia, the Russia of today. If you were present at a session of the Central Committee during the reading of an editorial in an English paper telling of the danger of the Soviet Union to Europe, you could hear Stalin exclaim triumphantly: 'Aha, at last they understand us!'

"Does Stalin believe in world revolution? He measures everything with money and bayonets. Once there is enough money, a sufficiency of strong bayonets, there will be a world revolution as a result of the victories of our armies and our gold. The little skirmishes which the Communist International now stages are but insignificant rehearsals for the impending tragedy. The great tragedy will come when our troops, the hordes of Eurasia, enter Berlin and Paris. Then Europe will cease being Europe and become part of Eurasia. Such is Stalin's faith in world revolution. He will present it to Europe on the tip of a Russian-Asiatic bayonet. And he will surrender to no western proletariat the hegemony of the revolution, for in the depths of his soul he hates and despises the proletariat of the West as much as he does its bourgeoisie.

"Is Stalin honest? Does he think of the needs and welfare of the people? I am deeply convinced that he aims at the happiness of the people, and sincerely regards himself as the incarnation of the toilers of the country. But what of it? Did not the Duke of Alba think that he labored for the people of the Netherlands, and was he not surprised when they rose in rebellion? And Nicholas I, the Iron Czar, did he not regard himself as the people's ruler, and was he not bewildered when the peasants revolted?

"Is it not, after all, an academic question, whether Stalin is honest or not? Of what avail is it that he does not steal, has no mistresses, indulges in no orgies, works hard? It does not make the people's burden lighter. In the end, it is how the people live, and not how Stalin does that counts.

"Stalin is a victim of the strangling, centralized bureaucracy which he himself has created. One recalls the horror with which Nicholas I exclaimed: 'Who said that I was the ruler of the country? The country is governed by my bureaucrats!' So far Stalin is the ruler; he sets the general course. But the basic force surrounding him consists of piratical adventurers, careerists who are waiting for Stalin to go, so that they may become the undivided masters of the land. Stalin restrains them. . . .

"Stalin is a blind power, with convictions. There is much in him that resembles Robespierre, with the difference that the latter was a European, Stalin an Asiatic. He has tightened the reins of the dictatorship to the extreme, and is entangled in them.

"If Stalin's regime of economic and political terror is for the happiness of humanity, I do not want that happiness. I am suffocating in the atmosphere he has created. I cannot and will not live and think while my head rests on the block of the guillotine."

Wars are often created by words rather than by deeds. Certain catchwords have been dinned in the ear of mankind for so long that it has become deaf to the voice of reason. If a generation has heard day in day out for twenty years the words Fascism, Communism, Socialism, Democracy; if these stock phrases are uttered by headlines and radio speeches by the hour, can you wonder that men, losing their power of judgment, should see only a flickering screen covered with changing colors before them, should hear only a shrilling of dissonances around them? After the four corners of the globe have been set on fire, the flames at last have seized the various state doctrines themselves and almost abolished the difference between them. Nowhere in the world may a state doctrine be found any more in its original form. All are in a stage of transition, and all are becoming more and more alike.

It is true that the citizen's security is, still today, far greater in the older democracies than in the autocracies. Daily life in America is easier, the citizen's rights are more protected, his freedom of speech and movement is greater than anywhere else. But everywhere the state has restricted these rights and diminished liberties of every kind. Mr. Bevin has the legal power to use the Archbishop of Canterbury as a coal miner. People seeing merely war measures in all this misunderstand the nature of this struggle which is nothing but a single great social revolution.

In what way does the economic freedom of a Russian, German, Italian differ from that of an American today? Obviously that of the latter is greater and, above all, guaranteed by laws protecting the citizen and favoring no party. Also the methods by which the state restricts competition and the accumulation of big fortunes are different.

But may the tire manufacturer in Detroit still fix the price of his merchandise? May the owner of copper mines in Salt Lake City take out as much as he pleases? May the Wall Street banker dispose of his profit in the way his father had done? Planned economy, first introduced by the Communists and then taken over by the Fascists, was applied also in the democracies a long time before the war had begun. Only twenty years ago England virtually expropriated its rich families by taxing their property up to 70 per cent. In Northumberland as well as in the Champagne, on the shores of the Thames and the Loire, nobility relinquished its beautiful homes before the first Nazi appeared on the Rhine, because taxes and upkeep had become prohibitive.

General equalization, containing so much justice and

destroying so much beauty, began in 1914. Then ended the nineteenth century which, beginning in 1789, had the exceptional duration of one hundred twenty-five years. It was not Communism that made the world barren: it was only the spirit of the age, trying to bridge the abyss between rich and poor, haves and havenots, that first manifested itself in the courageous and revolutionary attempts of the Bolshevists. In the same way the liberation from a master class, first initiated by the terrorism of the Jacobins, was later spread through the world in calmer and more deliberate fashion.

Then and now, in Paris and in Moscow, it was nothing but words that frightened the world. Not for the sake of the victims fallen in the first stage of the French and Russian revolutions did the heirs and traditionalists begin the struggle against both movements, just as little as the democracies of today have taken up the fight for the sake of the murdered, persecuted Jews and Christians. The old world wanted and still wants to protect itself against similar incursions, and to destroy the disturbers of peace. Men in calmer countries are frightened by such words as revolution, dictatorship, Bolshevism. But while they are restoring order, they are forced to adopt some of the measures inspired by the same doctrine which they are fighting. Hitler and Mussolini have taken over the planned economy of the same Bolshevists against whom they battled and, as time went on, have slipped more and more into the Bolshevistic course. The democracies, while fighting against these pupils

of the Russians, have allied themselves, amid inner misgivings, with the Bolsheviks, and are coming ever closer
to the same planned economy.

If the Russians had not at first excited the western world
with their slogans, the violent attempt to suppress them
would have been unnecessary, and a gradual development
might have equalized conditions without a further reign
of terror.

After the Bolshevists had seized power, two words filled
the air with their shrill sound for many years: Communism
and World Revolution. Men who had become accustomed
to the word Socialism and elected members of the Labor
party to every parliament and many governing posts, did
not understand that Communist aims were included in the
Socialist party programs and even identical with them.
Instead, the bourgeois world, with voluptuous shivering,
told the tale that everything in Russia was "common" to
all; that each received the same food, the same wages;
that religion and family had been abolished; that the
women belonged to everybody in common. Specially the
last item captivated the imagination of both sexes by its
suggestiveness.

The first two Internationals of 1864 and 1889, inspired
by Marx and by Jaurès, had almost the same program and
strove to achieve it with the same means as the one later
employed by Lenin. The difference lay in the fact that
only the latter succeeded in realizing the plan. But the
imagination of most men is not great enough to have any
conception of a Utopian program. When the sky is

radiant, nobody thinks of taking an overcoat along on a picnic; for it is surely not going to rain on such a bright day.

The word World Revolution was a veritable scarecrow. As if there had ever been a revolution in history aspiring to less! Each of them, like a new religion, gains pathos and passion through the feeling that it has been entrusted with a mission: We are the liberators of mankind! It had never been Lenin's dream to liberate only the Russian peasant. As his predecessors, Cromwell or Robespierre, he strove for the freedom of individual man everywhere in the world, trying to make him independent from the slave-holder who subjugates him and his children while hovering far above him in the clouds. Therefore Lenin and his followers shouted these wild words into space: "Liberty! World Revolution!"

When he founded the Third International in 1919, the bourgeois world shouted as one man: "The Russians want to meddle in the affairs of peace-loving countries!" As if creative thinkers with their books had not meddled as much in the affairs of other countries as powerful states do with their arms—and this for the last two thousand years! Did Christianity, did any new spiritual force keep away from the affairs of foreign countries? Have not the decisive victories of mankind been enforced by wars produced by just such influences? Propositions, protests, and demands are continuously gliding from the spiritual element into matter, from books to guns. This happened even if man was adjured by his spiritual preceptors not to shoot. Each great revolution, beginning with national need, has broadened into an international movement and later has again returned to nationalism.

The Russian Revolution paralyzed the citizen of other countries by the thousandfold repetition of its slogans. These became ever louder when the quarrel of the Russian leaders among themselves on the issue of world revolution excited foreign nations more and more. Under Lenin this issue was theoretical; he had his hands full if he wanted to save the Revolution in Russia. At that time several Russian leaders of bourgeois descent, like Tschitscherin and Krassin, declared that Russia was too weak to lead a world revolution; for the time being capitalism had the upper hand. The Bolshevists should be satisfied to influence others through their example, not through revolts.

At a later date this issue, before the eyes of the world, was brought to a head in the antagonism between Trotsky and Stalin. Socialism, said the former, could not be built up in one country alone. It certainly could, answered Stalin, and proved his point by developing industry in Russia during the next decade. When the Soviet Union became a military power under Stalin's leadership, rising simultaneously to the rank of an independent socialistic state, this would have tempted a Napoleonic character to seek great national victories under the guise of promoting world revolution.

It does credit to Stalin that such a turn did not take place. Of course, he has never buried his desire to see Socialism emerge as victor, nor restricted the Russian influence on older states. But he recognized that world revolution had been on the march for a long time without having to be created by the Bolshevists. When he "deferred" its outbreak at the congress of 1935, he reassured the capitalistic world, stressed his pacific intentions by joining the League of Nations, and yet did not give up one jot of his plans and ideas. The Trojan horse already stood inside the fortress of the Fascists. A year later Stalin made the following remarks during an interview with an American journalist:

"The belief that we are committed to world revolution is founded on a tragicomic misunderstanding. Though we believe that revolution will come to other countries, we do not expect it till everything is ready. Revolutions cannot be exported; each country will have to arrange these matters at its own convenience. We never had any intention of meddling in other people's countries and lives; all those stories are lies. Why should we bother about America? We give the same asylum to political emigrants as they do. Aren't there White Russians in the United States who are plotting against us? On the other hand, we give no refuge to terrorists. Thus America interprets the word asylum differently than we do. But that's all right, and we shan't complain. Of course, some people in your country have sympathy for us, and there are a few Americans among them; but others are on the side of the White Russians." The most interesting thing in this conversation is the explanatory adjective "tragicomic." It gives a profound insight into Stalin's character.

During the last twenty years, thousands of resounding words have conjured up for the old world the spectacle of world revolution in the style of a circus show: as if a Mongolian army, led by a motorized Genghis Khan, were marching west and, holding the busts of Marx and Lenin aloft, dragging Communism along in its wake. But in the meantime this arch criminal had built up his own country and transformed the Soviet Union into an industrialized state. There stood the frightened oil kings of London and Amsterdam who had to give up their Russian fields as lost; there stood the international bankers of New York and Paris, who had to forego repayment of those millions they had loaned to the Czar. Everyone wondered how these criminals could be discredited. Now they suddenly accused the Russians of not being communistic enough. The whole thing had been nothing but bluff. Non-Communists were treated far too well in Russia which was only masking its rampant nationalism. Their true purpose was said to be the same as that of old Russia: to conquer Constantinople. The only difference was that the new rulers had more chance to succeed.

The military power, which had to be built up in order to protect the young state from a second invasion by the old nations, was now represented as an aggressive weapon threatening the whole world. World revolution or nationalism: both positions equally infuriated Russia's enemies. And yet the perceptible transition investing Bolshevism with a national purpose should have reassured the world, had it not been misled by the distorted picture of the movement before its eyes. The slogan, "Imperialist," which should have been thrown on the rubbish pile a long time ago, but is still confusing people as much as the word, "Bolshevist," now took the place of the latter. The Russians, it was said, were striving for world dominion.

Has there ever been a revolution in which national aims have not been aspired to besides ideal ones? Cromwell, who wanted to liberate the souls of men—beginning with those of the English—also coveted Gibraltar and other strategic points. Danton wanted to have the Rhine for France. Stalin desired to establish a boundary line between Russia and Finland which would prevent any neighbor from shelling Leningrad. Neither by character nor training was he impelled to ape Napoleon. Russia is not the right starting point for such an undertaking. The Soviet Union is handicapped rather by too much than too little land; and it will take two more generations to develop the heritage left by the Czars to the Bolshevists.

If Stalin made Bolshevism more nationalistic than it had been under Lenin, he did so for two reasons: first, he wanted to furnish the international movement with a powerful foundation, an imposing center. Secondly, he wanted to deprive his enemies inside the country of the argument that they were governed by foreign theories favoring the invisible Third International. This modification of Stalin's policy merits approval instead of mockery. In the former Red Army the soldiers used to swear the following oath: "I, a son of the working people, will direct all my thoughts and deeds on the great aim of liberating all the workers." Now, in 1939, they swear: "I, citizen of the USSR, will sacrifice my blood for my people, my Soviet fatherland, and the government of workers and peasants."

This new outlook has been characterized as "Pan-Sovietism." Though we could have done without another "ism," at least this new slogan clarifies the difference between it and Pan-Slavism on the one, imperialism on the other hand.

This designation also points to the decisive difference between Russia's aims on the one hand and those of the Nazis on the other. We could condense it into one sentence: Hitler, according to his own words, wants to create a just balance between rich and poor nations by a new division of the world; Lenin and Stalin want to create a just balance between rich and poor classes.

But while Hitler demands world dominion for his German master race, Stalin has never aspired to similar aims for the people of the Soviet Union. The former foments world revolution through war, because this is the only means at a conqueror's disposal; the latter lets it ripen without war. Hitler prepared himself from the first day against an absolutely peaceable world which demanded nothing from Germany and had recognized her claims a long time before Hitler had appeared; Stalin prepared himself from the first day to defend his system against threatening assaults, especially from the German side. The former wants to make a new horizontal division of the world, the latter a vertical one.

HOW THE NAZIS IMITATE RUSSIA

The war spirit inspiring the Bolshevists at the time when the party was founded in 1903 and theoretically attempting to foment world revolution, has been absorbed forty years later by the construction of the first socialistic state, representing an isolated experiment. Only the ill will of those people who fear a growing tree as a competitor in the enjoyment of light, earth, and water, could see a defection from first principles in the new Russian development and ridicule the very thing that had frightened them before.

Fascism was the one adversary who, at least, did not deny its resemblance to the Moscow system. In another book I have quoted Mussolini's significant acknowledgment of the things he had learned from the Russians in the Duce's own words spoken to me. But the Nazis, though adopting not only the methods of the Russian secret police, but also a part of the Russian economic program, have twisted it around so much in their typical manner that it only sounds alike. The first thing Hitler proclaimed to his people in 1933 was "A Four Year Plan." Just as he imitated the whole fascistic apparatus—including the first of May celebrations, the gestures, the Roman greeting, even his own title of "Fuehrer"—he adopted the popularized word "Five Year Plan" from his so-called arch enemy, only changing it a little in order to prove his sovereignty.

Another thing that the Nazis did and that will make history laugh is the adoption of the Communist battle cry. Ley, the leader of the German workers, wrote in a manifesto of the year 1940: "Workers of all countries, unite—against English capitalism!" Such verbal tricks are fit only to amuse children or the diplomats belonging to a dying epoch. But the strangest thing is that this attempt at falsification contains a great truth: with each passing year the Nazis are becoming more and more Bolshevistic. Thus Ley spoke the truth as he went on: "National Socialism does not recognize the rule of money. In our society, business is regulated by the state assuming responsibility for everything. The state is independent of the stuffed purse."

The future outlook is already indicated by these similar principles. Just as many smaller trusts were combined into a few larger ones which could finally be taken over by the state, at a given moment the Russian track, to a certain extent drained of Communism, and the half Communist German one will be equalized so that the state engine will be able to roll beyond the border without any friction. This is going to be achieved by the fraternization of the uniformed workers in both armies.

The legends which the old world spread about Bolshevism are exactly the same which tried to kill "liberalism" a hundred years ago. A connecting line runs from the privileges of the nobility in the eighteenth century to the liberal ideas of the nineteenth, and the communistic ones of the twentieth, corresponding to the line leading from horse power to steam power, till this, in its turn, was superseded by electricity. What had first appeared as the political and technical ideas of tomorrow, has become that of yesterday. The liberal, once upon a time appearing as a long-haired revolutionary with soft, broad-brimmed hat, is now, at least in Europe, an old gentleman uttering a few obsolete thoughts, stemming from Manchester, in the style of a discarded engine in front of the newest streamliner.

Thus, if the legends about Bolshevism are not, or no longer true; if the word signifies neither general freedom nor general equality: what, then, is the Bolshevism of 1942?

It is a philosophy whereby each man is restrained from exploiting his neighbor and using the other's work and sweat for attaining those gifts of life forever out of the worker's reach. This society knows no classes, such as they virtually exist in all other countries, including the United States. Even here, though the poorest man may work his way up to the highest position and fortune, only a few are successful, while millions remain at the bottom. As long as raw materials and tools belong to private individuals, these may, by influencing a low price for labor and high price for their merchandise, become wealthy and bequeath to their children the means of cultivating spirit and mind. The laboring class, in Europe, has received an uneven share of the good things of life for the last hundred years: all members of the white collar class could attain wealth and luxury, while only a few could emerge from the second after overcoming immeasurable difficulties.

Bolshevism is a form of society under which the soil and the means of production belong to everyone alike, and the accident of birth makes the first start in life neither easier nor more difficult. If nobody works for the other man, but everybody for the community, then all are furnished with the same means: first the same education, later the same tools. The artisan is not obliged to save for ten years so that he may finally buy a small machine, but receives the best one at once. If the whole economic life is regulated and planned by the state, nobody may, by acquiring big factories and farms, buy the working capacity of a thousand men and thus attain power; but everybody may surpass the other through diligence and natural gifts, thus increasing his wages and being enabled to buy a more beautiful house and garden or car than his less efficient neighbor. Competition and ambition are not suppressed, but augmented. "Work," writes Stalin, "is no longer the heavy and profitless burden it used to be, but has become a matter of ambition and moral value."

Bolshevism is a form of society under which the private ownership of land and money is not eliminated, but permitted as recompense of one's own work. Even the accumulation of money and bequeathing of legacies is tolerated to a limited degree. Thus Bolshevism is more lenient than the system of the Essenes or early Christians who put all their belongings together so that each, regardless of his accomplishments, might receive the same food and clothing. Hundreds of kings, popes, and teachers have preached the Christian principle that each man was the son of God and his neighbor's brother; but all knew that they were lying. Now, for the first time, the attempt has been made to realize this principle on a large scale. A prelate is best qualified to testify in this case. Johnson, Dean of Canterbury, writes in his amazing book:

"At best, previously, a ladder had been let down by which the favored few of the 'lower order' might climb to privileged places among the privileged classes. The Russian program embraces 170 millions, taking into account the requirements of each individual through successive stages of life, as infant, as adolescent, as adult; in the sunshine of health and strength and in the shadows of sickness and old age. . . . This program claimed a warm welcome at the hands of Christians and scientists . . . from those who had for centuries preached about and prayed for just such an order based on just such principles."

Bolshevism is a form of society under which the poor man needs no charity, foundations, or scholarships to approach the sources of culture. He does not need these voluntary gifts of rich men, partly prompted by a good heart, partly by a feeling of fear and bad conscience. This puts an end to the feeling of shame felt by donor and recipient alike when they stand face to face. All forms of culture are gratuitously accessible to all citizens, and all plans of production regulated in such a way that each young man and woman earning their living have time and opportunity to study all those things at the universities—especially in technical schools—which they enjoy and which can advance them in their profession.

Bolshevism is a form of society under which the worker has to have no fear of sickness and old age—both nightmares making men helpless under every other system. Nobody is subjected to the ignominious necessity of asking others for help at this stage: the state supports everyone who is not able to work. As there are no private owners and no economic depressions, there is no unemployment, which other states can eliminate only in war time. Strikes, forbidden in Fascist countries, have become impossible; the same is true of picketing and moral compulsion. Each citizen is entitled to a two weeks' vacation with full pay. Women receive their full wages without working before and after childbirth.

Bolshevism is a form of society under which no child less than fourteen may work instead of growing and studying; and anyone under sixteen only in special cases. It is a form of society under which everyone is working seven hours a day, reduced to six in the case of dangerous occupations. For 80 per cent of the workers every sixth day is free, for the other 20 per cent every fifth. All this is true only in peace time. Here no pyramid has been constructed as in Fascist countries; and therefore all fear of the boss and hate against the boss is eliminated. As the director of each factory is only a technical leader, each workman may elect a representative for the Communist leadership. The latter may dismiss no one without good reason, as businessmen in the establishments of the old world may still do at will, though the workers are partly protected by unions. The council of Russian workers may force higher officials to dismiss the director.

Bolshevism is a form of society under which just as many cliques and intrigues may persist as in any other circle. But as nobody is able to accumulate a fortune or collect money without working, the chief organ of corruption is not powerful enough to provide privileges for the single individual. No superior official or editor may be bribed as in Europe. All feelings of hate and envy still prevalent in the old world must die out and be replaced by new ones only flourishing among us under the stress of a general disaster. The Dean of Canterbury uttered the significant judgment: "Materially the Soviets are steadily rising, morally the ascent is still steeper."

Bolshevism is a form of society under which, as was proven in the last fourteen years, a rising standard of life was made possible—and this for everybody. Taking 1929, the beginning of reconstruction after wars and famines, as a point of departure, the wages in the Soviet Union have mounted in eight years from 100 to 371. In contrast, they have been decreased in America and Germany to 86 and 79 per cent, respectively. At the same time, the productive capacity of Soviet industry has mounted from 100 to 841 per cent, while it barely increased in capitalistic countries or even dropped to lower figures.

Bolshevism is a form of society under which technicians and inventors have been seized by new ambitions and driven to new achievements. "The plants and research laboratories for airplanes are larger than in the West," writes the President of the Curtiss Wright Company, "because they have the whole resources of the state at their disposal. Engineers and designers have an opportunity for expansive work that no private company could afford." "The Russian engineer has new opportunities," writes the chief engineer of Metro-Vickers in Sheffield. "The business principles of our industries in the West often force the engineer to dissipate his energy and knowledge to no purpose. New orders are solicited by every English firm working in the same field; each hurries to make new drawings, but all except one are wasted. In Russia, the engineer knows that his designs will be used if they are good. Planned economy lets him see the fruits of his work—and that's the thing that counts."

Bolshevism is a form of society under which no race or color, religion or language, fill a member of any group with fear that he will be persecuted or be at a disadvantage. As there is not only one official language in the Union—as little as in Switzerland—the prejudice of a nationalism deeming its own language and country the best in the world becomes doubly apparent. As each race is entitled to its own culture, foreign habits are eagerly studied and often adopted. It was possible to combine eleven states with more than a hundred races and languages only because the laws of the Soviets correspond to philosophy and the universal tendencies of mankind. Of course, there are contrasts as everywhere else: even Lincoln, who liberated the Negroes, declared that he had no desire to marry a Negress. Where the state makes such enormous demands on men as in the Soviet Union, it must give a feeling of security to the citizen in exchange and may erect no scale resembling the one used by the Nazis even inside their own country to divide the whole people into supermen and lower men, so that no normal person seems to exist there any more.

Bolshevism is a form of society under which no exchange, no speculators, no quotation of stocks and bonds may persist. It excludes persons who make their living and become alternately rich and poor by buying shares of industrial establishments whose products they have never seen and to whose maintenance they have not contributed one whit: ordinary gamblers. These unproductive creatures, a detriment to the state whether they win or lose, cannot persist in a community which has replaced lucky chances by achievements, speculation using the labor of others by one's own labor or, to put it briefly, money by labor.

Bolshevism is a form of society under which creative people, specially the engineer and the artist, receive full benefit for all they have thought out or produced. The state itself, excluding all middlemen, offers the work of talented men for sale without deriving any profit from this transaction. The inventor is not dependent on a financier or war profiteer who has earned millions on the stock exchange, and needs no sponsor to gain money and leisure for the execution of his project. It is the state that provides him with raw materials, tools, and laboratories and buys the completed invention at as unusual a price as is merited by a creative genius. On the other hand, the author is caught in the dilemma of being allowed to write only what befits the doctrines of the new state. The writer—and especially the philosopher and historian—though most generously remunerated, is torn by a moral conflict.

Bolshevism is a form of society under which the equal rights of women have been guaranteed by the constitution itself. Freedom to marry is greater than in most other countries, and as everyone is earning money—otherwise he could not eat—and as both partners are generally earning at the same time, there is no obstacle to early marriages. Abortion was permitted by law in the times of Lenin; later it was abolished. This was the only step back made by Stalin. The principles of the dictator, that a nation must produce as many children as possible to have more soldiers, apparently took the encircled Soviets like a panic. Nevertheless the annihilation of this world-historical progress is unexcusable.

Lenin was opposed to every sexual laxity and spoke his mind in this phrase: "What normal man would, under normal circumstances, cover himself with filth and drink from a puddle? Or even from a glass whose edge has been soiled by many lips?" A divorce is easily obtained if one of the partners desires it; but frequent divorces are condemned by public opinion. Father and mother must both provide for the children, a divorced wife also for a former husband if he is stricken by illness and not sufficiently taken care of by the state. Thirty-three per cent of all workers in the Soviet Union are women who have made a place for themselves in every profession: half of all the physicians, one-fourth of all scientific research workers, nine-tenths of all the school teachers. As community kitchens have been installed in country and town, and machinery as well as special domestic workers help in the household, each woman is able to continue her studies during her leisure hours and to think of the good of the state. The highest

Soviet has 189 female members. In no other country and at no other time has woman been drawn so much into politics: one of the marked contrasts to the Fascist system.

Bolshevism is a form of society under which a superior injuring the health of his workers exposes himself to the most severe punishment. Other major crimes are profiteering, manipulation of chain stores, wasting of seed corn, speculating of any kind. The number of prisoners has been reduced by half, because most of the convicted persons are taken to open colonies where they are reformed, generally within a period of two months. Also forced labor is not imposed for more than a year. Sixty-five per cent of all condemned persons are not confined in prisons. They receive the greater part of the wages earned by their labor, for nobody in the Soviet Union may work for nothing. The convicts elect a soviet whose president decides on all infractions of discipline. Special prison dress and solitary confinement have been abolished. Every prisoner is allowed to smoke after work or play a musical instrument. Only one thing has been forbidden that the Czars allowed in their prisons: card games.

Bolshevism is a form of society under which the former collaboration of Czar and Church for the purpose of maintaining their privileges and preserving the ignorance of the masses has come to an end. Separation of state, church, and school, as well as freedom of antireligious propaganda, are the same in the Soviet Union as in the United States. The Church may teach within the family circle, but not proselytize by means of press and radio. Each may avow his faith and convert others. No one is hindered from hanging an ikon on his wall.

"Marx, Lenin, and Stalin," writes the unimpeachable Dean of Canterbury, "were antireligious just because they believed that religion has constantly allied itself with organized injustice. Outrages were committed, as the church has become corrupt and wealthy, neglectful not only of social justice, liberty, education of the masses, and social welfare in general, but also actively prosecuting those who made these things their concern. It is not natural for people to murder priests. . . . It is totally untrue to say that the present day Soviets lack religious freedom. . . . Communism in its positive aspect is no fundamental enemy of religion, least of all of the Christian religion. In the long run, it will prove to be a true friend in at least one essential particular. It provides Socialism with a new moral base and is in process of achieving on the "this-world" level those very things that we Christians have to often profess with our lips but deny with our lives. It has struck the death blow to an immoral order which we have tacitly accepted.

"Had Christians from the first but given to Communists the welcome which was due to men whose motto—'from everyone according to his ability and to everyone according to his need'—is so wholly Christian, and who had passed from words to deeds in their construction of a concrete order based on these principles, Christians would have done more honor to the intention of their founder, and

Soviet Communists might never have felt compelled to launch their war against religion."

Thus Bolshevism is a form of society under which as great a part of personal life is sacrificed to the community as under Fascism; it is not its purpose, however, to create or elevate certain races, but to abolish classes or hinder them to arise. It is a philosophy deifying the state as much as that of the Fascists; it is not its purpose, however, to establish world dominion outside its boundaries and rule over other nations, but to give security to the individual inside its boundaries and brighten his life: an anti-hero system for the good of the multitude.

Two of the three tenets of the French Revolution—not carried out by their originators—have been realized: Equality and Fraternity. Liberty not. It is limited because of the external needs of the state and the internal coercion forcing everyone to accept the ruling state philosophy. But, in contrast with most revolutions, these three articles of faith are being more, and not less, honored as time goes on. In Moscow, where the first national assembly had been dissolved, general and secret franchise was granted to the people twenty years later. Once the war has been won, the victory over Germany and the alliance with the western powers, it is to be hoped, will diminish tension to such a degree that the individual citizen will be able gradually to enjoy the liberty guaranteed to him by the constitution.

With none of its neighbors has Russia lived in as great an amity as with Germany, though the common boundary line of the two countries was very long before Poland became independent. For five hundred years no Russian had fired on a German. The only exception was one war against Prussia—and then the Czar was an ally of Austria. The Russians were allied with Austria in three major wars, though they fought six times against the Turks and many times against their other neighbors. Therefore the Russians were hated nowhere in Germany—if only for the reason that the two people did not know each other. While German will to power, passion, and romanticism was directed, for a thousand years, against the West, against France, and national ambition was bled white on ever new battlefields, there were no wars and conflicts in the East, against Russia. The Romanovs maintained this peaceful policy for three hundred years, till they finally fought against Germany in the World War and met with defeat.

The attempt to continue the war during the first stage of the revolution of 1917 failed immediately; for the soldiers in the trenches had already begun to fraternize on this front.

This feeling of friendship was stressed after the Bolshevists had appeared on the scene. On the second day after his assumption of power, Trotsky broadcast his famous first message to the world, and especially to Germany. This was one of the first times that the radio was used to transmit speeches to distant countries. The appeal, beginning with the words "To All" made a deep impression after three years of war. The listening world heard these words: "We propose that all nations and governments at war should enter into immediate negotiations for the purpose of establishing a democratic and just peace without annexations and reparations."

During the next four years, the relations between Russia and Germany were settled at three green conference tables: first as between victor and vanquished; then as between neutrals; finally in the form of an alliance.

The first of these tables was probably not green, but a rough piece of furniture standing in a dilapidated inn of the half-demolished town, Brest Litowsk. Here the victorious German generals met the defeated Bolshevists on Christmas, 1917. An immortal scene! The Germans, already beset by a presentiment of future disaster, but still appearing as victors with their resplendent medals, clanking sabers and spurs, and resounding voices—were here confronted by half a dozen Communists, workers and literary men with shabby coats and somber but determined faces, ready to foot the bill for the Czarist mismanagement which they had just destroyed. Here these Prussian generals, whose external power was still recognized in half of Europe, these heirs of a caste privileged through the centuries, looked with their haughty and cold glances into the intellectual and passionate faces of revolutionaries who were proletarians and idealists, fighters and fanatics. To their terror, the spruce generals saw even one or two women among the delegates and could hardly suppress their laughter. Both parties despised each other; but the blustering victors, whose leaders pounded the table with their fists at the critical moment, knew their decline was at hand.

Nobody recognized the precariousness of the German situation more quickly than Lenin. "The more the Germans advance," he said, "the clearer it becomes to all, even to many German citizens themselves, that the war offers no way out. The more their troops advance, the more the army, which despoils helpless people like a robber band and steals their last morsel of food despite their sullen resistance, becomes imperiled." Today, after twenty-four years, Lenin's successor, Stalin, could predict the same thing to the Kaiser's successor word for word. Later, after the defeat, Lenin summed up the German campaign in his magnificent style: "At first the balloon swelled up till it had covered three-fourths of Europe. Then it burst; and nothing remined behind except an evil stench."

A year later, in the spring of 1919, German delegates sat in the Weimar theater deliberating on the Versailles treaty to which they had been subjected. Here, however, there were neither German generals nor Russian revolutionaries. The former had run away after the defeat, the latter had not been invited to attend this council. At that time destiny confronted the Germans with a question testing their character more deeply than any other one ever posed by history: they were offered the choice between liberty and property. The miracle had happened that the great Russian army had been eliminated in the middle of the war and now was ready to fight on the German side. The powerful victors in Paris were trembling. Secret reports of those days, made accessible only now, speak of the frightening possibility that the two defeated powers, Russia and Germany, might unite themselves overnight and force the exhausted allied armies to fresh battles.

But the Russian savior, who could have redeemed the Germans from their desperate plight, was a Bolshevist. The bourgeois Germans—including the Socialists, who adhered to the dogma but not to the methods of the Russians—feared nothing so much as this diabolical word. Though the Bolshevists wanted to march with, and not against Germany, and the German-Russian war of liberation in 1813 might have been repeated, the Germans preferred security of life and money to liberation and signed the treaty of Versailles.

In one of Genoa's marvelous Renaissance palaces the leaders of Europe sat together again three years later, in the spring of 1923, at a huge U-shaped table: victors all of them, but with such tired faces that they looked vanquished. The allies of yesterday mistrusted and hated each other: there was discord between the nations, and even between statesmen of the same countries. Above all, they were sulking because the interest of the world was not centered on them, but on the representatives of the two great conquered nations, Russia and Germany.

The German representative was taller than most of the others. A man of the world with polished manners, an accomplished linguist speaking more languages than anyone else there, he was the most highly cultured person I ever met among my contemporaries. It was the same Walther Rathenau who had evolved the idea of planned economy in tangible form and thus taught the Russians a piece of their own technique. For the last few months he had been Foreign Minister of the German Republic. The other man was short, resembling Lenin in some points. He, too, was a man of high culture, proficient in several languages, and familiar with European problems: Tschitscherin, Foreign Minister of Soviet Russia, which soon afterward expanded into the Soviet Union. He was assisted by Krassin, an astute merchant who knew how to talk business to Rathenau.

The conference looked at these two delegates as distrustfully as conservative English society would have looked at two attractive damsels of easy virtue smuggled surreptitiously into its midst. After three years of boycott they had been finally admitted to this highly moral circle. The whole world expected that they would misbehave.

They did misbehave. Recognizing that the victors intended to cheat, or at least separate them, they stole a march on the others and concluded a sudden alliance. The ex-

plosion was terrific and almost blew up the whole conference. At the close of this momentous Easter day
Rathenau said to me: "I took over Germany such as it
was. Herr Ludendorff had lost the war. Russia is our only
possible ally. I couldn't have concluded the pact before.
Afterward it would have been too late. Today was the only
time."

Through this daring pact of Rapallo, Rathenau demonstrated a statesmanship not experienced in Germany since
Bismarck's days. In retribution, he was murdered soon
afterward by the same Nazis who concluded a similar pact
with Moscow seventeen years later.

After this pact, the two newly allied nations were driven
to entirely different policies by their systems and circumstances. The Russians, intent on internal reconstruction,
thought of no conquests. The Germans, opposing the new
political system and boycotting the republic in overwhelming majority, thought of nothing but revenge and re-
demption of their losses. The heirs of the Czar, convinced
of his guilt and the justice of the Russian defeat, refused
to pay the debts of the old regime and preferred to start
something new. The heirs of the Kaiser continuously complained that they were being cheated by the victors—and
also a part of their fellow countrymen—and paid a fortune
to the ruler who had run away.

Yet, two forces in Germany tried to strengthen the alliance with Russia: the big trusts, especially the electric
companies, saw at that time—before the Five Year Plans—
opportunities for big business deals in Russia; the general

staff had visions of a German-Russian military combination. Both were attracted by the huge quantities of raw materials and men to be found in Russia, while the Russians admired the German precision and that superior quality of the foreign product which they could not match at that time. The German generals admired—first secretly and then openly—the victories of the Red Army over the troops of the interventionists. Both parties, though prompted by different reasons, opposed the peace of Versailles.

Their original misgivings were overcome by the amazing reliability of their allies. The Bolshevists promptly honored the drafts of the Germans. Lenin's saying that "the old Russian cart should be attached to the modern German dynamo" seemed to promise enormous profits. The German general staff, while helping to build up the Russian army, ferreted out some valuable information and imagined that the Russians weren't up to their tricks. The leader of this policy was General von Seeckt who had created a small German army soon after Trotsky had created a big Russian one.

Seeckt represents one of the exceptional figures produced by the Prussian general staff if this ancient Junker caste is rejuvenated by the admittance of an official's son belonging to the new nobility. A highly cultured man with a philosophic and even aesthetic bent, he was one of the most interesting officers in the German army since the days of General von Schlieffen. In every way, he presented a sharp contrast to Field Marshal von Hindenburg whom he despised and who, in his turn, revenged himself by dismissing Seeckt.

The main difference between the two new armies lay in the mentality of the soldiers. For the unemployed Germans, soldiering was a job whereby they could earn their daily bread. Very few thought of revenge. This thought was much more firmly entrenched in the old German bourgeoisie than in the new army. On the other hand, the Russians resembled Cromwell's "Army of Saints" who had not always behaved in saintly fashion. Both nations made a virtue of necessity.

Besides the industrialists and the general staff, the first Nazis were interested in the Russian alliance and liked to be called National-Bolshevists instead of National-Socialists. Roehm, also Goebbels and Himmler, at that time young adventurers, dabbled in Russian politics long before they came into power. Their thought, "Together we shall be invincible," was correct. But they forgot to add: "If we adopt the same economic system."

This German-Russian amity was symbolized in the twenties by two statesmen who used to meet in Moscow in unusual places and at unusual hours. Tschitscherin, the Russian Foreign Minister, and Count Brockdorff-Rantzau, the German ambassador, both liked to get up in the afternoon, drink in the evening, and work at night. This peculiarity kept Rantzau away from his own embassy, where he appeared only once during his stay in Moscow. Both cultured men of the world, independent and gifted, they had received a violent shock through the disintegration of their respective empires, though both had recognized the weaknesses of the last rulers and courts, and the Russian had gone over to the new party some time ago. Count Rantzau invariably called Wilhelm the imperial deserter.

At that time two eminent Americans correctly diagnosed the most important problem of the age. Bullitt, the later ambassador, had already predicted the stability of the Soviet regime in 1919 after a short trip to Russia. Unfortunately the report he made to President Wilson during the Versailles conference was ignored. Ten years later Secretary of State Stimson, in a classic exposé, warned the British government not to furnish Japan with war materials, because such a precedent would shatter the moral force of the League of Nations. What a tragic and ironic spectacle to see this prescient man fight Japan today with the sword instead of the pen!

Since the beginning of Stalin's dictatorship, his state has been threatened by no one so much as the Germans. Nevertheless, as he confirmed to me, the memory of the old cordial relationship between the two nations was still in his heart: "If there is one nation to which we are attracted —to the whole people or at least to a majority—they are the Germans." And when I asked why, he answered: "It's a fact." He had a correct insight into that German mixture of obedience and brutality, both of which only wait for the word of command. He told me, in this connection, the following anecdote:

"When I was in Berlin in 1907, we had arranged that the Socialists of every part of the city should get together at a big meeting. About two hundred had come from the suburbs. When they came to the railroad gate where the tickets had to be handed over, the ticket collector was not there. We Russians who were among them urged them to pass through the open gate, as they all had their railroad tickets; but they would not budge, and it looked as if they would have waited there for hours if the ticket collector had not happened to turn up. When I was in Dresden I found that the law was treated with the same respect as frost or thunder or some other natural force against which man's will is of no avail. When I was in Vienna in 1912 I went with my Russian friends into the park at Schönbrunn; we noticed everywhere the sign *Verboten,* but we were not used to such things and we must have paid a fine of a *krone* twenty times over for the pleasure of breaking the law. Our German friends laughed at us for our delight in that form of amusement. That's how it was in those days.

"But today? Where is the German sense of order today? Where is the respect for law? The Nazis break the law whenever they find it stands in their way. They shoot and bludgeon right and left."

All the Five Year Plans had been conceived in anticipation of a German attack. The same anticipation prompted Stalin to look for future allies in the West. What is happening today has been prepared by him for a long time, though in a devious way and with variable luck.

Stalin tried for fifteen years to gain England's confidence. When the British recognized the Soviets in 1924, seven years after their foundation, they did this with utmost reluctance and for the only reason that they were jealous of the German competition which had conquered the Russian market. The influence of the big antisocialist businessmen was so great that war in 1926 was prevented only by the intervention of the great statesman, Lord Balfour. A forged letter made it possible to break off relations for three years. Then Stalin denounced England as decadent—a term applied by all revolutionaries to old states, and by youths of original mind to old gentlemen. From 1924 to 1934 Stalin could not count on an English alliance against Germany. When Chamberlain, who considered Hitler as a shield against the Soviets, became Prime Minister, Stalin gave up the whole thing. He saw how England furnished Japan with war materials, after pursuing a policy in Spain which, according to the Dean of Canterbury, amounted to murdering the legal Spanish government.

Stalin's attempts to win the sympathy of France—the starting point of Communism—were more dramatic. The only foreign flag in Soviet Russia is an old Communard banner of the Paris Commune of 1871, draped over Lenin's glass coffin. And the Czarist alliance joining Russia and France for twenty years against Germany had never been forgotten. In Paris everything seemed possible, for the internal opposition there was more passionate than in England. Though the power of the Paris bankers, who wanted the return of their loans to the former Czar at any cost and demanded a *cordon sanitaire* round the Soviet Union, seemed to grow, Stalin foresaw with pleasure that corruption would eventually kill French capitalism. Then Herriot came to Moscow and afterward wrote a brilliant book in favor of the Soviets. The relations with Czechoslovakia were even more propitious.

With Italy, dogmatically the arch enemy of Bolshevism, Stalin concluded a pact of friendship in 1933, though Pope and King were against the atheistic Soviets. The conflicting interests were so much emphasized through the Spanish concussion that Mussolini did not dare to proclaim the new so-called friendship with Hitler at that time.

Stalin had to be lenient with Japan while his arms were still weak, and even sacrificed the Eastern-Chinese railway. He did this also for the purpose of increasing the friction between Japan and the United States. The change of their respective positions is shown through the fact that in 1932 the Japanese refused a pact proposed by Stalin, while in 1940 Stalin could refuse a pact proposed by Japan. The building up of Central Asia for the purposes of war and peace affords the protection to Stalin in the East without which he could not fight against Germany today. In the meantime there occurred the trial of strength in the summer of 1938, known as the "Chang-Ku-Feng Incident." This was a real battle with modern weapons "amid deepest peace" in which 18,000 Japanese were supposed to have been killed—a number exceeding that of the warriors fallen in the famous battles of antiquity.

While, on all sides, corrupt diplomats let themselves be pushed around by threatening events, Stalin did two things: He joined the League of Nations and doubled his armaments. Thus, in one breath, he avowed and denied an ideal—just as the League of Nations itself had done for the last fifteen years. Such turns prove that a statesman is worth his salt. The League of Nations, called by Lenin a gathering of thieves, and looked on by Stalin and all of Russia in a similar way for eight years, now seemed the fitting instrument for addressing the nations from the Geneva rostrum. He wanted to talk to the people over the heads of their governments, just as Trotsky had done at the time of the peace negotiations with Germany. Thus he hoped to effect a change in the prevailing sentiments and possibly overthrow the pro-Nazi governments of Paris and London.

When the first Russian appeared in Geneva in 1928, all the bourgeois diplomats were frightened to death. This was not because a somber Bolshevist of half-Asiatic descent threatened with war and revolution, but because a not at all somber man of western culture disappointed everybody by suggesting nothing less than general disarmament. This was Maxim Litvinoff. A few years older than Stalin, he had run away from his bourgeois home at twenty-two, become a revolutionary, had been exiled by the Czars five times to Siberia and escaped again, been driven out of Paris, had become a teacher of languages in Amsterdam, studied English life and politics, married the revolutionary daughter of a respectable English bourgeois family. Thus he was familiar with western culture, but separated from its political forms. For twelve years he virtually carried out Stalin's foreign policies, partly inspiring and frequently directing them. If Stalin trusts a collaborator—which happens but seldom—he begrudges him neither glory nor appreciation.

It was not a formal session of the League but the Disarmament Conference into which Litvinoff hurled his maiden speech with its thunder and lightning, pathos and irony: a surprise and a masterpiece. At that time the defamation of Bolshevism and the prejudice of the whole world stood in full bloom. Though it is customary that a newcomer in parliament should take a backseat for several years and listen to the others, this disturbing intruder burst into speech the first day:

"Gentlemen, why debate any more? Thirty sessions have conferred on disarmament, fourteen committees have met one hundred twenty times, one hundred eleven resolutions have been taken. But what has been accomplished by all this trouble and these stacks of paper? Absolutely nothing. We are just where we were before. This kind of business must stop." General consternation. The great Fridtjof Nansen, who had occasionally raised the League to heights to which it never aspired by itself, had been the only one to talk in a similar way to these cautious diplomats. But Nansen had stood alone. Now this Russian suddenly showed his cards and urged full disarmament:

"The Soviet government is ready to abolish every

weapon if the other states pass the same resolution. Therefore we ask whether they are willing to do so. We want an answer, immediately, without committees. Our proposition is perfectly plain." This was a piece of marvelous propaganda for the proletarians of all countries, and a terrible shock for the armaments makers of all countries. When the British delegate answered that the Russians were fomenting civil war everywhere, his voice sank to a whisper. A few years later Lord Londonderry was still indignant over this immoral demand of the Russians. Whereas former kings liked to emphasize that the people must not be deprived of their religion, the British delegate emphasized that the people must not be deprived of their bombs.

In the following years Litvinoff, as Stalin's representative, became more and more aggressive. At his side fought Titulescu, founder of the Little Entente and one of the most illustrious figures of the period between the two world wars, and so was his friend and ally, Benes of Czechoslovakia. These two proved that the smallest nations could produce the biggest men. As Nansen and Briand were dead, Litvinoff was the most powerful man among those with a moral purpose. Even in 1932, when Germany was already preparing her attack, the Russian demanded the abolition of all major weapons. The list he produced ten years ago staggers our imagination today: prohibition of tanks, heavy guns, naval guns over 12 inches, aircraft carriers, battleships over 10,000 tons, heavy bombers, all kinds of aerial bombs, chemical warfare, aerial weapons of any kind.

Litvinoff, though achieving no tangible results, gained a moral victory for the Soviets in Geneva. But if it was supposedly an easy thing to shoot such fireworks which were bound to burst in mid-air, why did no other state dare to make similar propositions? Because all of them were controlled by the private interests of armament makers. Litvinoff used no biblical pathos, and made no mention of Christianity. At this green table, enveloped by the deference due to all the courts of Europe, he blurted out his speeches in a tart and often cynical tone. "The Japanese," he said, "will go on and on; the signatories of the Kellogg pact will disregard their obligations. The press is subservient to different interests in different countries, and also caters to capitalistic groups and private individuals. Our conception of security differs from that of others who only talk of security if someone attacks them. The Soviets want to do away with war, because it ruins both victors and vanquished. After ten years of debating, people have not even begun to understand what the Soviets want."

Soon afterward he said: "Is this the time for the delegates to go home, convinced that they have done their whole duty? Now when a bloody war, or rather a series of bloody wars, is threatening every continent and the whole world? Which state can be sure that it will be exempt? Some may get caught sooner, some later, but there is no escape. Imperialistic states, intent on conquest and growth of their might, invariably begin by attacking a single objective. But once their appetites have been satisfied in this direction, they turn to other objectives, and generally to all of them." Prophetic words which nobody wanted to believe in the Geneva of 1934.

When Hitler left the League in the first year of his rule, the whole people cheered. The Germans had felt as uncomfortable there as a generation ago at the Hague Tribunal. Stresemann, who had sacrificed his health to bring Germany into the League, had been an honest, conservative man; but even his closest advisers belonged to a different class. If Germany's entrance into the League had been farcical, her departure was sincerely heartfelt. Any institution denying the religion of violence is suspect to the Germans. The present author, who wrote in favor of a League as early as during the first World War, was attacked by everybody.

Then, in the winter of 1933-1934, the House of Delegates in Geneva involuntarily became a House of God for one moment: it became the temple of Janus in which an open door signified war, a closed one peace. Hitler walked out of one door, Stalin came in through the other. This virtual synchronization is the aptest symbol of the deep abyss between Nazis and Soviets. When the Russians joined the League, Litvinoff gave one of his classic speeches which began neither with tears of joy nor with blessings:

"A new state with a new system has always been subjected to hostility. The old world, flinging itself on the Soviets, has tried to stifle us. Many believed that eternal peace were at hand, if one could only get rid of the Soviets. We are not specially impressed by the League of Nations, because we ourselves are a League of 200 nations. Peace among so many races inside one state is a new thing in history and only possible because the Soviets are not interested in nationalistic or racial ideas. What is that highly praised peace organization aspired to by the League? Political slogans age very quickly. If they have been repeated too often without being realized, they must be filled with new content and rejuvenated."

When the question of the Soviet debts was scheduled for one of the sessions, it was suggested to elect an "impartial" personage to preside at this meeting. Litvinoff answered: "Only the angels are impartial. Here are two worlds, capitalists and Soviet. There may be a third one in heaven among the angels. But I am afraid that none of them would be available for the League."

Starting with mockery, the Russian went on to productive work. Litvinoff coined the word, "indivisible peace," fought for collective security, and continuously attacked the Japanese sitting across the table. It was he who defined the word "Aggressor" and obtained, together with Titulescu, the signature of a majority of countries who guaranteed to fight said aggressor. The following actions were defined as aggression: Declaration of war; invasion; attack on land, sea, or air; blockade; aid extended to armed bands operating in foreign countries; refusal to call such bands back. An attack could not be justified under the following pretenses: political or social structure of a state; simulation of bad economic conditions; disturbances through strikes, revolutions, civil wars; violations of the rights of a foreign state; violation of frontiers. A complete list of all the pretenses under which Hitler justified his conquests six years later before the German people.

At that time, round 1933, the so-called postwar period was changing into the prewar period all over the world. The League, abandoned by the Germans and joined by the Russians, was morally recognized by the United States, which thus made symbolic amends for her former defection. Litvinoff, the bridge builder between Russia and Geneva, was equally successful in Washington, where the Russians, not recognized for 16 years, had been under a moral ban. Today, ten years later, he is again able to unite the war aims of the great capitalistic and the great anti-capitalistic power.

Whereas the speeches of some statesmen seem so empty to anyone reading them today that their initial success seems inconceivable, those of others gain, like fine wines, body and aroma with the years. Litvinoff's Geneva speeches seemed less amazing in the thirties than today.

"The Soviet government," he said in 1935, "opposes every system of colonies, spheres of influence, or imperialistic conceptions of any kind. The League should be nothing but a permanent peace conference and a warning to every aggressor." Or at another time: "The passivity of the League caused the attack on Abyssinia. The leniency shown this aggressor encouraged others to the Spanish experiment. Lack of assistance to Spain led to the attack on China: three cases in five years. Resolute interference in one case would have saved us all further trouble; everybody would have seen that an attack does not pay." When the Soviets proposed in 1938 to agree on collective action against every aggression, England refused to sign. And, when the Russians helped the Czechs at that time, Lord Londonderry proposed that, in case of war, England, instead of marching with the Czechs, should go with Hitler. Finally the last attempt of the Soviets in March 1939 to prevent the war by calling a conference was frustrated by England which considered such a meeting as "premature."

Premature in the eyes of the British Tories, who also determined French politics, were all other resolutions passed against Hitler at a time when he was ready to start. History will make the Chamberlain government—unless one wants to go back to his predecessor, Baldwin—responsible for the postponement of the present British-Russian alliance from 1939 to 1941. The hate of these two conservative businessmen who had both entered the field of politics as graybeards; the natural aversion of these ingrained capitalists—who had become rich through this system—against anything smacking of Bolshevism was so great that they misjudged Hitler and considered him their champion in the war against radicalism.

As in a drama, these narrow-minded men of yesterday are overshadowed by a great man of today who by a tragic development may not be the leader of tomorrow. For eight years Churchill, a member of their own party, had fought against these two leaders of British politics in his Catonian speeches. He, who had used his sword against the Soviets while the two others were still deeply immersed in the wool-and-steel trade, had learned to understand the present age. Though he retained his conservative views—or rather returned to them—he recognized that, of the two movements seemingly endangering the world, only the German one would cause general disaster. Thus Churchill, rejuvenating himself, worked for an alliance with Russia. In vain. His adversaries had the upper hand.

In the same clear-cut way, the socially minded men in Paris separated themselves from the money-minded ones. But there were also people like Bonnet and Laval—the one on the scene and the other behind it—who fought against Blum, Cot, Mandel. The only difference was that the French Bonnets were after the money, while the English were honest.

Chamberlain's bids for Hitler's favor at the expense of the Czechs and world peace—too recent and well known to be recapitulated here—necessarily provoked the merciless criticism of the Soviets. Though every spectator realized that England, unprepared as she was, had to give in; it was equally obvious that the governments of Chamberlain and Baldwin were to blame for this state of affairs and the frustration of the Russian alliance. Baldwin went so far as to make light of Hitler's armaments. Afterward he told the House that he had been obliged to speak like this because the elections were coming up and otherwise his party might have been defeated. Fundamentally, the actions of these two men were motivated by their capitalistic world view. Churchill was able to adapt his conservative principles to the conceptions of a higher sphere. His outlook, unlike that of his two predecessors, was not hedged in by considerations of money.

The polite king of little Albania neatly summarized the European problem: "There are two madmen in Europe who drive everybody crazy. Besides, there are two damned fools, Chamberlain and Daladier, who are asleep." But they weren't asleep. The turn of affairs in Munich caused Litvinoff's downfall. Dismissed by Stalin, he was held in reserve for the future. Europe, League of Nations, war against aggression: this program had exhausted itself and was being replaced by what the Russians called "the Munich alliance between the Fascists and the imperialistic clique in London and Paris." Also the Balkan states toppled over and had to lean more or less on the Fascist victors. Poland, which had flirted with Hitler far too long, fell into one swoon after the other. The Czechs were the only ones who still stuck to Russia. Stalin felt that he was being encircled by Japan and Germany, perhaps also by Poland. Already three years earlier Hitler had publicly shouted in Nuremberg: "If I had the Urals, Siberia, the Ukraine with their wealth of precious metals, wheat and forests, we could revel in riches. We shall conquer, under the Swastika." (It was one of his tricks to omit the word "them" after "conquer.")

Finally the German conquest of Prague, which frightened even the British Prime Minister, seemed to pave the way for an alliance with Russia. Not only the conservative Churchill, but also Lloyd-George, the old Liberal, urged this pact—though both men had been enemies of the

Soviets. It was a desperate plea for help that Lloyd-George sent out: "An alliance, an agreement, a pact, it does not matter what it is called. With Russia you have overwhelming forces which Germany with her army cannot stand up against."

But Chamberlain began the negotiations to which he had been forced half-heartedly and with a bad conscience. He evidently did not wish to get any results. Instead of flying himself to Stalin as he had flown thrice to Hitler, he sent a subordinate on a slow boat. The trip, which could have been made in twelve hours, took two weeks. Also Lord Halifax was too fine a gentleman to transport his top hat into the land of caps. The British propositions, never published in detail, probably asked Stalin to guarantee the security of Eastern Poland. Then, answered Stalin, the Nazis would march against the Baltic states, which were not protected by English pledges. Consequently these would have to be safeguarded against German attacks. The negotiations were drawn out for so long that Lloyd-George publicly ridiculed the tempo.

Stalin sent another warning through Molotov in June '39: "Though we are negotiating with the West, we have never stopped trading with Germany and Italy." Bluff, they said in London. Hadn't Hitler called the Soviets bloody swine and scum of the earth just a short time ago? Wasn't it Chamberlain's master plan to divert Germany from her colonial dreams and entice her with thoughts of Russian booty?

Suddenly Stalin, the arch enemy of culture, was being

courted from two sides. At that time the gigantic German war machine had already burst upon everyone's sight. It stood there whirring softly like a car whose motor had been started and which is only waiting for the gear shift to dash off. England, in the face of this threatening machine, finally forgot her old prejudices. "Our natural interests," said Churchill, "unite us with Russia. Rumania, Poland, the Baltic states will feel safer if Russia stands behind them." And Lloyd-George added: "The Russians are the only ones able to help the Poles, provided we help them at the same time."

Similar words were heard in Moscow. As late as August 1, 1939, an official paper wrote: "It is 25 years ago since the Germans set out to destroy their enemies at one stroke. They vanquished three-fourths of Europe. Then the balloon was deflated. Today their position is worse. Germany enters the war in a weakened economic condition and will be derided as aggressor by the whole world."

But in the meantime the Nazis had begun to tone down their vituperations against Russia and finally cut them out altogether. Molotov had been in Berlin and been treated with special courtesy by the arch enemy. It was told that, after his return to Moscow, the German ambassador handed him a present for Stalin: phonograph records secretly made of the conversations at the Munich parley and reproducing Chamberlain's voice at the moment when he incited Hitler to fight against Russia. The same British government, which had offended Stalin personally by the way it had carried on the Moscow negotiations, offered the

German agent, Wohltat, a loan up to four billion dollars so that Hitler could arm a little more against England. As late as May 1939, Chamberlain recommended to the House of Commons a pact with Hitler, in whom his astute glance had recognized a gentleman during three days of conferences. On the fifth he refused a pact with Russia.

In more passionate countries Chamberlain would have been differently treated. The plea to spare a dead man should be advanced by no one who wants to write history: they are all dead, her subjects. Baldwin and Chamberlain, who helped Hitler—their champion against the Soviets—for eight years, are to blame for the fact that England was not prepared.

Stalin was, during these weeks, in the position of an elderly bachelor continuously threatened by a dangerous woman in his neighborhood who wants to marry him and become the boss. When he finally wants to get rid of her by marrying someone else, the bride-elect, vaunting her own virtue in contrast to her suitor's dark past, suddenly withdraws. Thus, fully convinced that he will be the final victor, he is forced, at this critical moment, to fall into the arms of his grim neighbor in order to clarify the case once for all through a temporary marriage.

Practical considerations were an added incentive. How could the English, who had always refused to make plans for a joint campaign, send troops to Poland? Wouldn't he, Stalin, have to fight for the Poles by himself? And why should he protect Poland, which had always treated him with suspicion? Why should he make a pact with England which hated and continuously offended him? On the other hand, a pact with Hitler could perhaps procure temporary peace for him during which he could increase his armaments and improve his frontiers. If Hitler was busy in the West, he, as his ally, could possibly advance and regain, without fighting, the old frontiers lost by Russia in the world war. Perhaps the miracle would happen that Stalin could keep his newly reconstructed country entirely out of the war, while the capitalistic powers bloodied each other's noses.

On August 25, 1939, the pact between Hitler and Stalin was signed in Moscow: no alliance but a nonaggression pact. On the photograph showing the signatories Stalin stands at the back, revealing by an Asiatic grin his opinion of this friendship. There are wedding photos in which the bridegroom grins in this way.

The honeymoon was the most farcical one known to modern history. The idyl lasted not only a few weeks, but two years. "If a rupture is to come," wrote Max Werner in his prophetic book *Battle for the World*, "both parties will be able to choose the opportune moment." Hitler profited as much by this temporary arrangement as Stalin. As both had entered the agreement with the intention to betray each other, it was fundamentally an honest deal.

Hitler, while ignoring the positive teachings of Bismarck, had been taught only a negative thing from his great predecessor: the fear of a two-front war. He had also been taught the precept not to fight England under any condition and confirmed it in his book. (One shouldn't believe the story that the book was written by someone else; no other German could have murdered his language like this.) Therefore Hitler, in concluding this pact, was on the right track and might have won, if he had stuck to it. The only disadvantage was that he ceased to be St. George slaying the Bolshevik dragon for the benefit of all decent men.

In the short time during which this idyl lasted, the newlyweds plied each other with gifts. Hitler, who suddenly wanted to impress the world with the might of the same Soviets whom he had belittled just before, announced that the arrival of certain supplies sent by boat from Leningrad to Kiel meant "more than a victorious battle; they guarantee victory." Stalin, in his turn, profited still more when he marched into Poland and advanced his frontiers westward, almost without fighting. After the atrocities of the Nazis it was easy for the Reds to assume the part of a savior. Everywhere, on the Bug and the San, Stalin improved his frontiers in order to resist his new friend more successfully in the future.

The great benefit accruing to the world and allied victory from Stalin's pact, has been divulged by Hitler himself. Later in their speeches of June 23, 1941, Hitler and Ribbentrop set forth that it was Stalin who prevented an attack on England in the fall of 1940: the wicked Russians, cried Hitler in his familiar sniveling manner, had occupied Bessarabia and thus set the Balkans in motion against Germany. Yes, Hitler himself confessed in his declaration of war that he did not dare attack England in the rear if he had to confront an armed Russia. This sentence would be sufficient to justify every opponent of Hitler—in other words, the majority of mankind—in giving thanks to Stalin.

Presumably both Stalin and Hitler perused the reports of their general staffs on the preparations in the newly acquired frontier zones of their respective countries with frigid and stubborn smiles. If Hitler had the railway tracks in Poland repaired, Stalin understood that his enemy-friend was preparing them for future use against himself. If Stalin demanded more land in the Carpathian mountains, or simply took it, Hitler understood that these annexations intended to hinder his future attack. Possibly both became pale when looking at the new map: now for the first time these two gigantic armies and countries stood opposite each other—without being separated by a shock-absorber—from the Baltic to the Black Sea. They resembled two rope-dancers who, throwing and catching balls, advance toward each other on the same rope without knowing which of the two will get out of the way. The only ones daring to smile in this situation were the five German journalists who had appeared in Moscow after having been ordered for ten years by their "Fuehrer" to abuse Russia more effectively by spitting on it.

But the law of dictatorship drives the conqueror ever onward, even farther than he wants to go. Hitler's boundless ambition impelled him—at a moment when he was not threatened by Stalin—to beat the other to it. Nobody forced him to this action, least of all the German people. Here is his only point of resemblance with Napoleon, to whom he can be otherwise compared in no feature of his character, life, or activity. The only thing the two have in common is this fateful necessity. Also in 1812 the Emperor could have stayed quietly at home and ruled in peace, had not the demonic ambition of the upstart, who considers peace as tantamount to defeat, impelled him on. No famine, no threat, no demand of the people drove Hitler against Russia. Only his demon. Though emphasizing the desperate danger of a war on two fronts in his book, he deliberately undertook a campaign which is going to cause his collapse.

The reasons which speak for Stalin's resistance consist mostly of moral factors.

The opening up of the country's natural resources is responsible for only one half of this success; the other half must be credited to the new state. Stalin could not have created his tank and airplane factories, he could not have produced his capable officers, he could not have scored either a material or a moral success without the enthusiastic co-operation of a liberated youth. If we except the bombing of England, we shall not find a similar unity of army and people in our time. A comparison with the Germans makes this very clear.

The Germans have set out to conquer that which they do not need; the Russians want to save that which they need. The Germans have set out to win world dominion for a race whose superiority they inwardly doubt; the Russians want to maintain a state system in which they believe. The Germans set out to achieve victory under the same authoritarian forms which led them to defeat twenty-five years ago. The Russians want to affirm, for themselves and the world, a new state form. The Germans, with whom obedience is a passion, are an ancient warrior people which marches blindly forward wherever the leader commands; the Russians are protecting their native soil, which they themselves have only just acquired.

The Germans fight with regular armies in foreign climates and foreign lands; the Russians, guerrillas and regulars alike, fight among familiar landscapes amid familiar conditions. The Germans are held together by discipline and by discipline alone, for they have never been enemies of Russia; the Russians have been preparing themselves with the utmost devotion. The Germans obey as their fathers obeyed, and their generals of today still have the aristocratic Junker names which headed the imperial armies; the Russians obey the commands of men who are all sons of workers and peasants.

The Russian leader is a general who received the highest military decoration from Lenin in 1919 with the following testimony: "In a moment of great danger, near Krassnaja, Joseph Stalin, through his untiring energy, saved the tottering Red Army. Fighting himself in the front line, he inspired the soldiers through his example." The German leader is also a general, though he did not even become a sergeant during four years of war, and though nothing of his heroic deeds is recorded in his thick book except the history of his regiment before he joined it.

Not the strength and number of tanks or planes will decide the issue. The old Prussian obedience may perhaps suffice for the conquest of Europe; it will not suffice to hold Europe down in the long run. This tells the whole story of why the Germans will not defeat the Russians.

The alliance of Russia and America is by no means artificial or merely prompted by need; it was their long estrangement which was artificial.

The American and the Russian of today are very similar: Both have an admiration for speed and sport, but an aversion to war. Both believe in numbers, percentages, polls. Both standardize life and love. Both prefer movement to rest and do not look for privacy. But they differ definitely from the angle of money.

Whereas the two countries, so far away from each other, have little opportunity to get together, nature has joined them symbolically in surprising manner: everything lacked by one country for war purposes is owned by the other. Manganese, chromite, potash, and mercury, lacked by America, may be obtained from the Soviet Union. The latter receives copper, which it lacks, from America. The cultivated districts in both countries stand almost in the same ratio to the number of inhabitants: 367 million acres in the Soviet Union, 327 in the United States, which figures correspond closely to the proportion of inhabitants: 182 to 132 millions.

On the other hand, the standard of life is entirely different. Production in America is ten times as great per head as in Russia. Metal production in the Soviet Union is not even a third as high per head as it has been in the United States for a long time. Coal production in the Soviet Union only amounts to 7% of world production, while in America it reaches 68%. The merchant marine of the Soviets amounted, before the war, to ½% of world tonnage, in America to 22%. But both countries have more empty space than all other places of the world. Whereas the Soviet Union has 11 and America 41 inhabitants to the square mile, Germany has 363 and England 668.

No Russian has ever expressed greater sympathy for the United States than Stalin. He wrote:

"If Leninism is a school, the study of theory and practice is characterized by two peculiarities, namely: revolutionary zeal, inspired by the Russian spirit and businesslike practicality, inspired by the American spirit. Revolutionary zeal is the antidote to laziness, routinism, conservatism, apathy of thought, slavish adherence to tradition and to the belief of our forefathers. Revolutionary zeal is a life-giving force that stimulates thought, spurs on to action, throws the outworn into the limbo of forgotten things, and opens the portals of the future. Without such zeal there can be no advance. But it has a drawback, seeing that in practice it tends to vent itself in revolutionary talk, unless it is intimately combined with level-headedness and businesslike action imbued with the American spirit.

"The best antidote to revolutionary fantasy is practical work imbued with the American spirit. Such businesslike, practical endeavor is an unquenchable force, one that recognizes no obstacles, one that, by sheer common sense, thrusts aside everything which might impede progress, one that invariably carries a thing once embarked upon to completion (even though the affair may seem a puny one), one without which any genuine work of construction is impossible.

"But the practical, businesslike American spirit is liable to degenerate into narrow-minded, unprincipled commercialism, if it be not allied with revolutionary zeal. In party and government work, a combination of the Russian revolutionary zeal with the practical American spirit is the essence of Leninism."

In order to understand this statement more fully, I asked Stalin how it was possible that the most capitalistic country was admired so much by the antipode, the Socialist state.

Without a moment's pause, Stalin gave a magnificent answer: "You are overstating things. Here there is no general respect for everything that is American. There is only a respect for the American sense of practicality in everything, in industry, in literature, and in business; but we never forget that it is a capitalist land. They are sound people, or at least there are many sound people there, sound in mind as well as in body, sound in their whole attitude toward work and toward everyday facts. The practical business side of American life and its simplicity has our sympathy. In spite of its capitalistic character, the customs which are in vogue throughout the industrial and economic life of America are more democratic than in any European country, for in Europe the influence of the aristocracy is not yet obliterated."

"You do not know how true that is," I said in an undertone. But the interpreter heard me and translated it for Stalin.

"Yes, I know," answered Stalin. "In spite of the fact that the feudal form of government has been wiped out in many European lands, the feudal spirit still remains and is powerful. From the aristocratic hang-over many technicians and specialists carry on the tradition of their origin. That cannot be said of America. It is a land of colonists without a landed gentry or an aristocracy, and hence the simple vigor of its customs. In industry and business they are simple, and our workmen who have become leaders of industry here notice that fact immediately when they go to America. There it is difficult to distinguish between the engineer and the simple workman while they are at their job."

Here Stalin had formulated with simplicity and sureness of insight the parallel between those two utterly different nations, America and Russia.

When I visited him in 1931, he had no reason to express this sympathy. This was the time before the United States had recognized the Soviets. In those days he was no "Man of Destiny."

Today he has earned this title. Yet even then his rich life was replete with so much activity that I doubted whether this man with his realism, his rows of figures and percentages believed in destiny. "Do you believe in Fate?" I asked.

He became very serious. He turned to me and looked me straight in the face. Then, after a tense pause, he said: "No, I do not believe in Fate. That is simply a prejudice. It is a nonsensical idea." He laughed in his dark muffled way and said in German, *"Schicksal, Schicksal."* Then he reverted to his native language and said: "Just as with the Greeks. They had their gods and goddesses who directed everything from above."

"You have been through a hundred dangers," I said, "when you were banned and exiled, in revolutions and in wars. Is it merely an accident that you were not killed and that someone else is not in your place today?"

He was somewhat annoyed, but only for a moment. Then he said, in a clear, ringing voice:

"No accident. Probably there were inner and outer causes that prevented my death. But it could have happened by accident that someone else might be sitting here and not I."

And as if he wished to break through this dense and annoying cloud and get back to his Hegelian clarity, he said: "Fate is contrary to law. It is something mystic. In this mystical thing I do not believe. Of course there were causes why I came through all these dangers. It could not have happened merely by accident."

Schicksal (Fate)! The echoes of that mighty German

word were still in my ears as we took our seats in the waiting motor car.

In this citadel the Czars lived and ruled, sometimes wielding a power that had not been arrived at by natural means. And here Death found them. Everything around us gleamed sinister in the dusk—sinister and embattled. And here the son of the Georgian peasant had laughed defiantly when the word *Destiny* was mentioned. The ring of cannons in the forecourt reflected the evening light in a dull sheen. But on each muzzle glittered brightly the letter *N,* embossed in gold—the superscription which a little corporal from a barren island had dared to stamp on the mouth of Death. "What have you still to do with Destiny?" Napoleon said to Goethe. "Politics are DESTINY."

CHRONOLOGY

1879	Joseph Dzugashvili (Stalin) born in Georgia.
1893	Stalin enters the Orthodox Seminary in Tiflis.
1897	Stalin, expelled from the Seminary, becomes a Socialist.
1902	For the first time arrested, in Batum.
1903-1913	Stalin six times captured by the Czarist Okhrana and sent to Siberia; he meets Lenin at a Party Congress in Finland.
1904-1905	Russo-Japanese War. Workers' Revolution in Russia collapses.
1905	Czar Nicholas II issues a manifesto promising democratic liberties and a legislative assembly (Duma). Stalin in underground St. Petersburg.
1905-1909	Period of "liberalization" in Russia.
1907	Stalin in Tiflis.
1913	Stalin in Siberia.
1914	In Monasterskoye (Siberia) Stalin receives Lenin's theses on the War.
1917	February Revolution in Russia. Lenin, Trotsky, Stalin return from exile. October Revolution; overthrow of the liberal Kerensky Government.
1918	Lenin's First Soviet Constitution. Trotsky's peace negotiations with Germany, Brest-Litovsk.

CHRONOLOGY

1918-1920	Civil War in Russia. Foreign Intervention. Commissar Stalin in command in the Ukraine, in the Donetz Basin, against Poland, etc. Stalin victorious at Tsaritsyn (Stalingrad) and Kharkov.
1922	Stalin General Secretary of the Communist Party.
1924	(January 22) Lenin's death. Second Soviet Constitution.
1925-1927	Stalin's fight against Trotsky and "Trotsky-ism." Trotsky exiled and ordered to leave the U.S.S.R.
1928-1932	Period of Industrialization. Stalin's Five Year Plan.
1933	Hitler Dictator in Germany. Stalin's Second Five Year Plan.
1935	Stakhanov Movement.
1936	Stalin's Constitution of the U.S.S.R.
1937	Moscow trials.
1938	Japan forced back, at Chang-Ku-Feng. Stalin's Third Five Year Plan. Russia excluded from Munich Parley.
1939	Moscow Pact between the U.S.S.R. and Germany (August 25). Russo-Finnish War.
1940	Occupation of Bessarabia.
1941	Hitler attacks Russia. Stalin Defense Commissar.

INDEX

INDEX

INDEX

INDEX

INDEX

INDEX